Lauren Kay

101 RELAXING COLORING BOOK

THIS BOOK BELONGS TO

TEST COLOR PAGE

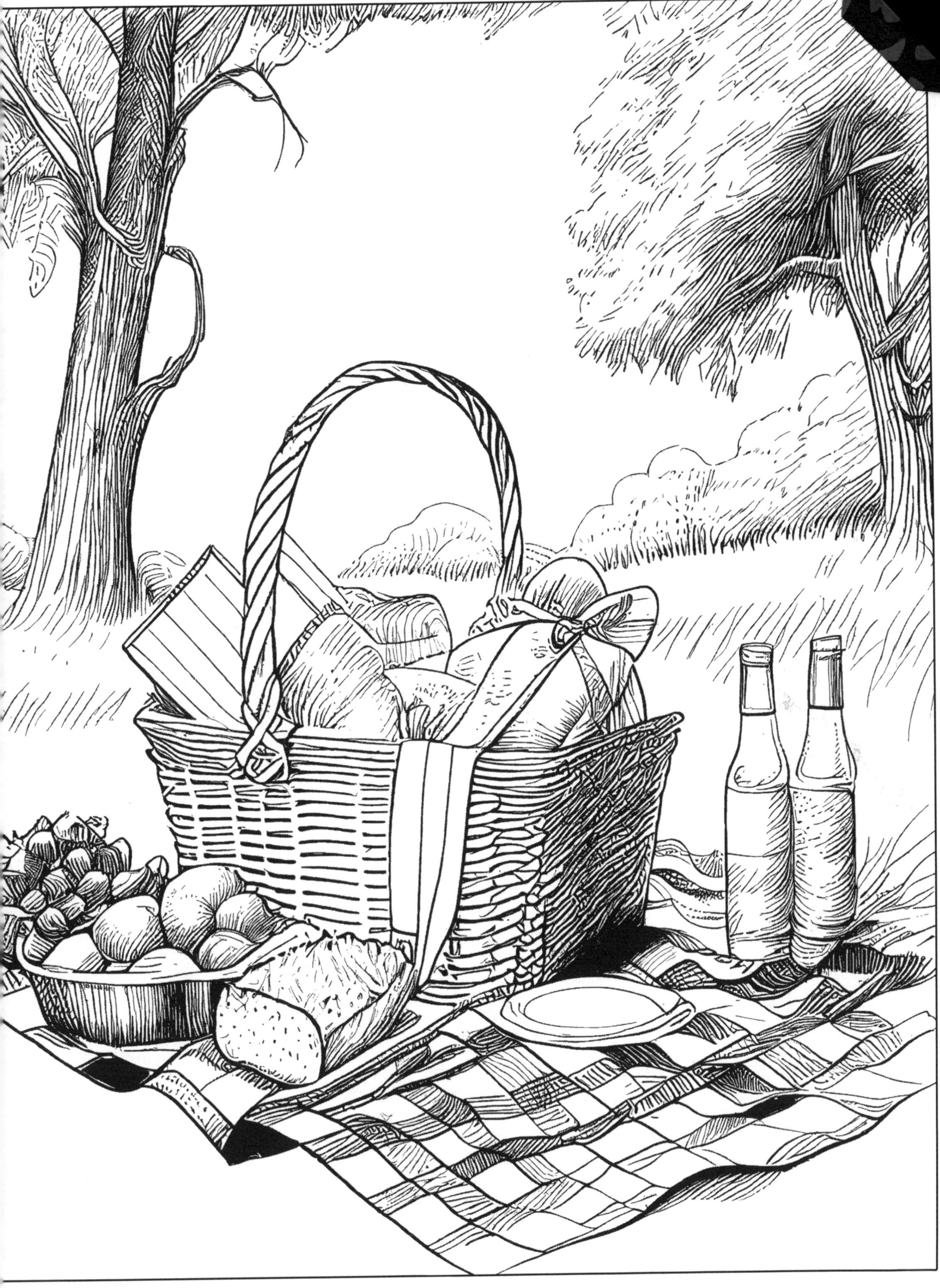

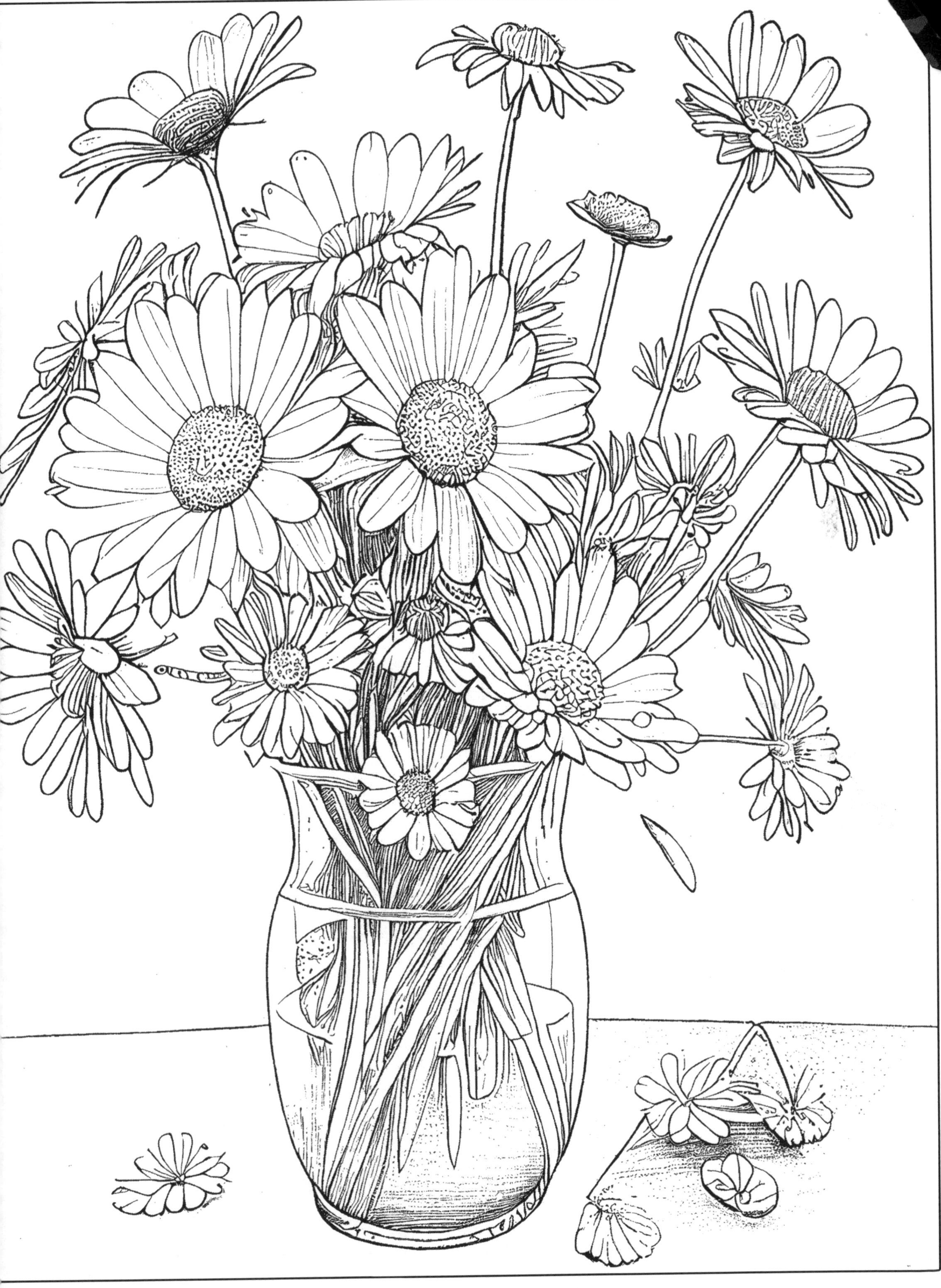

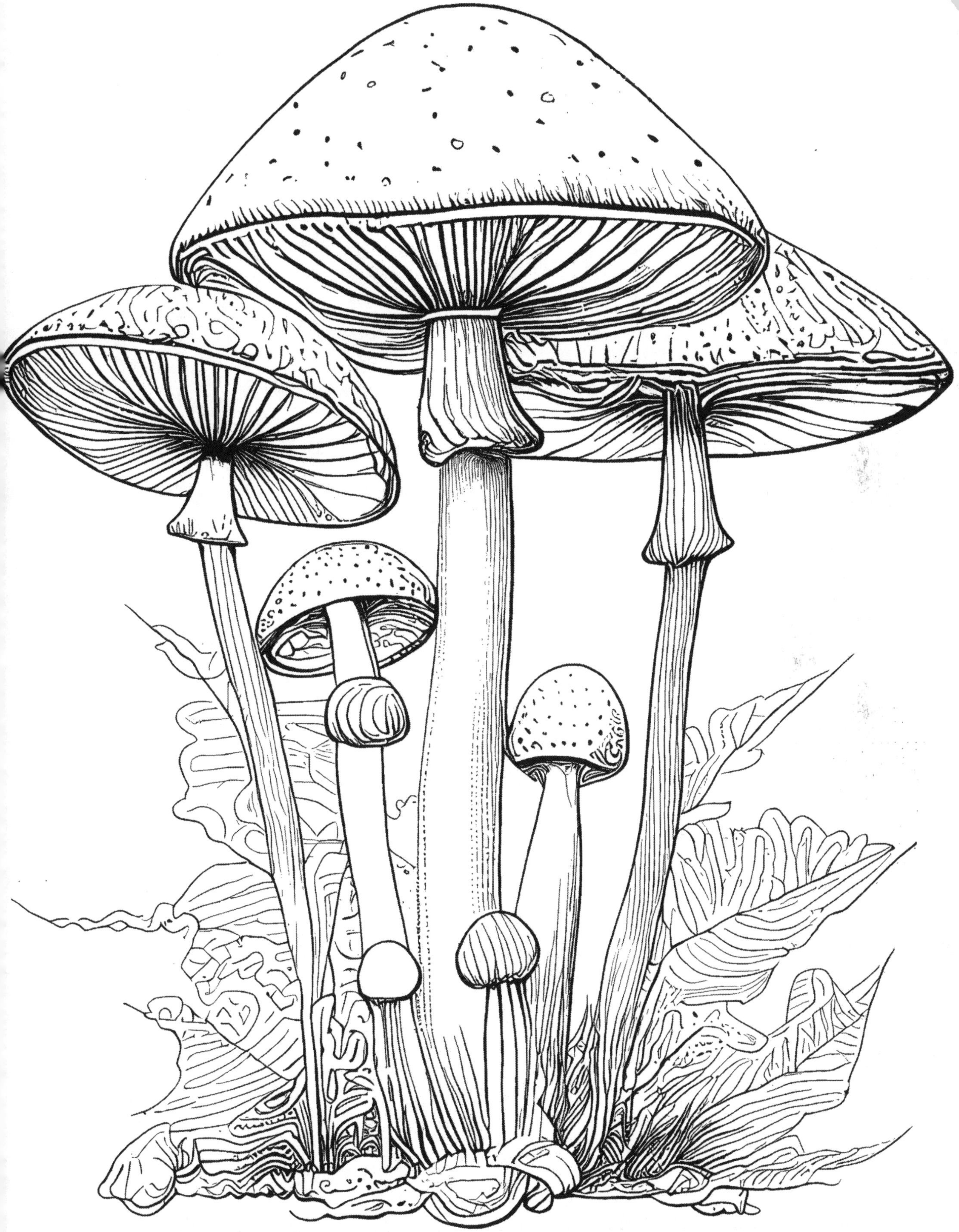

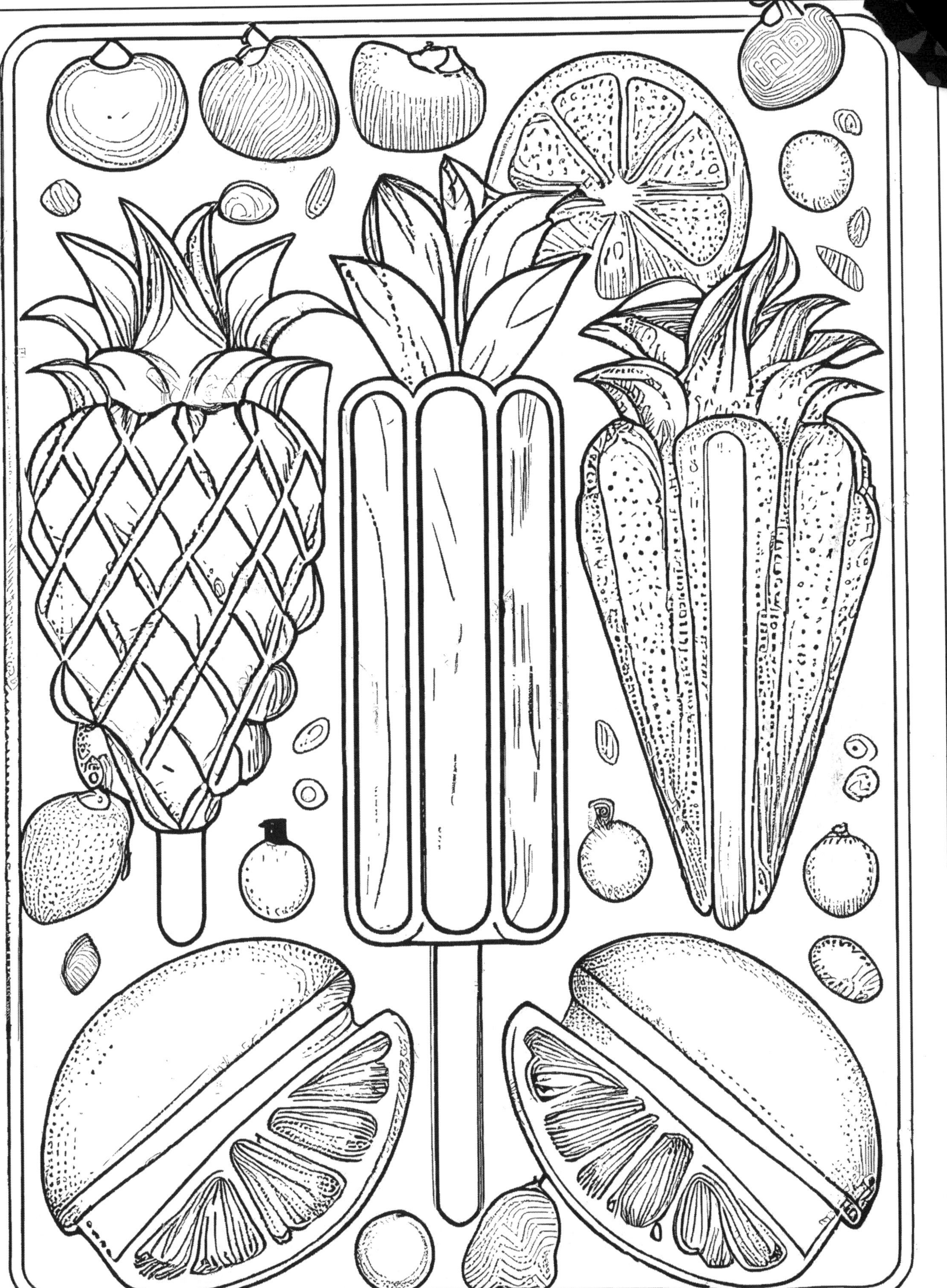

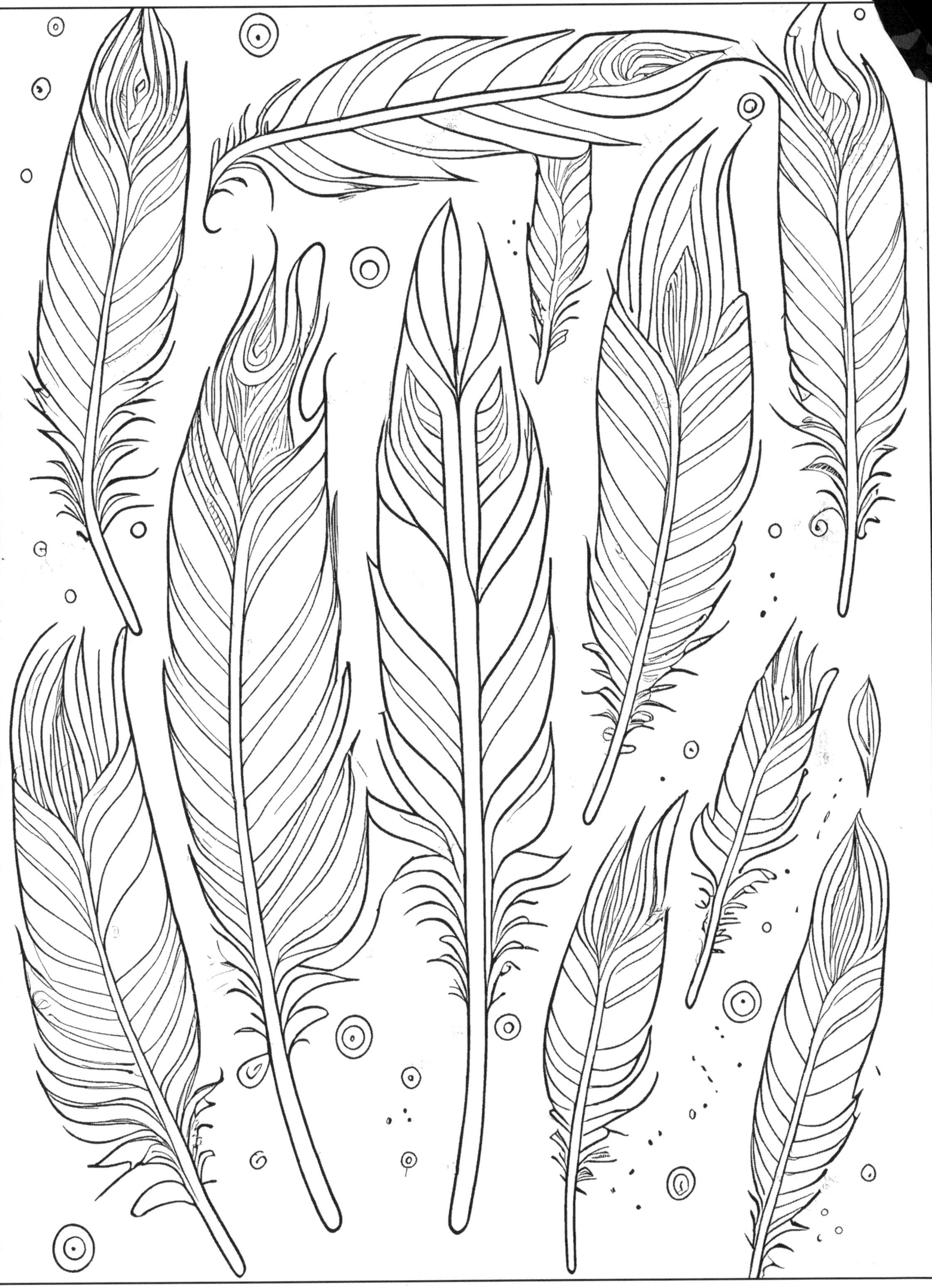

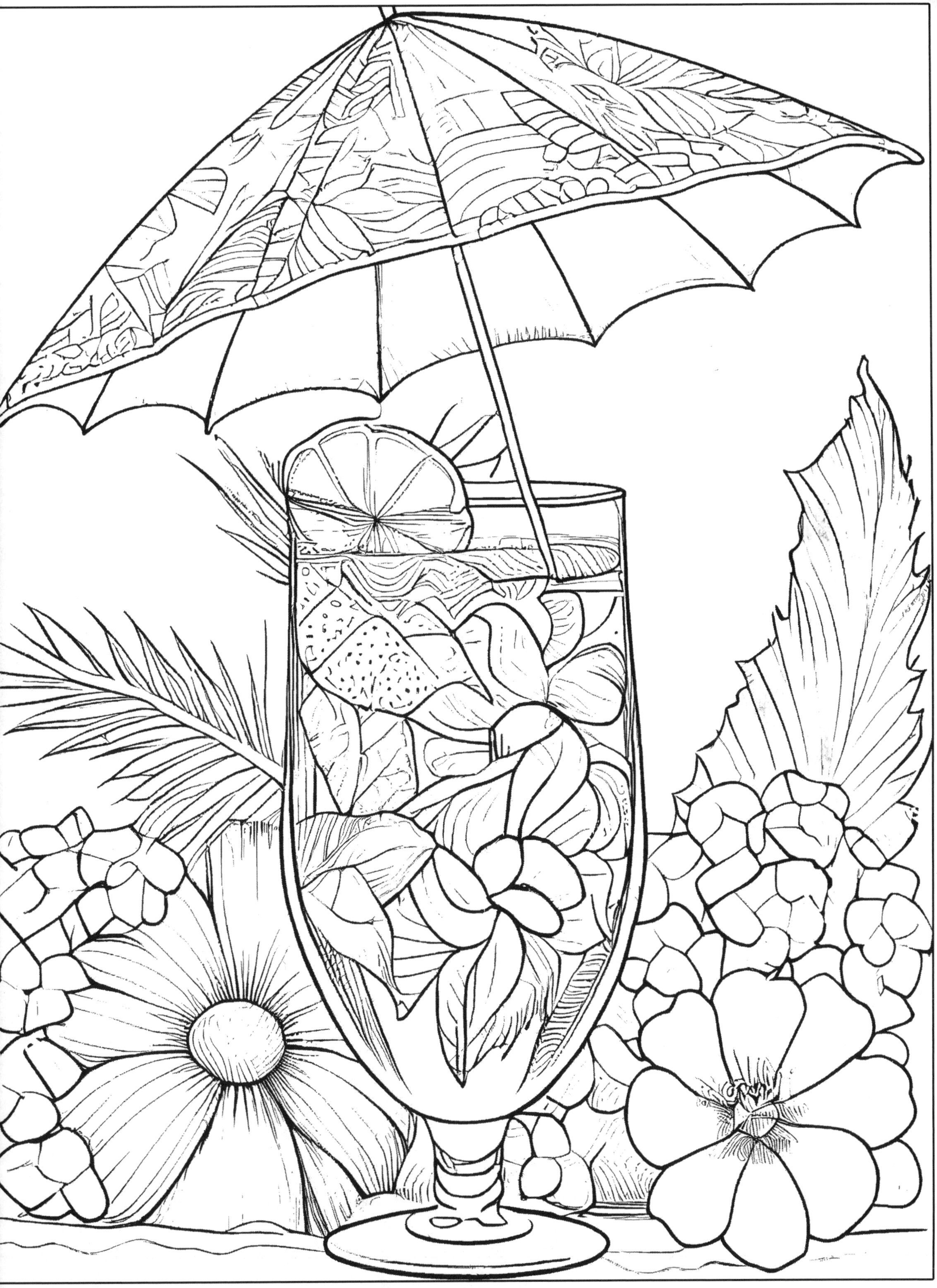

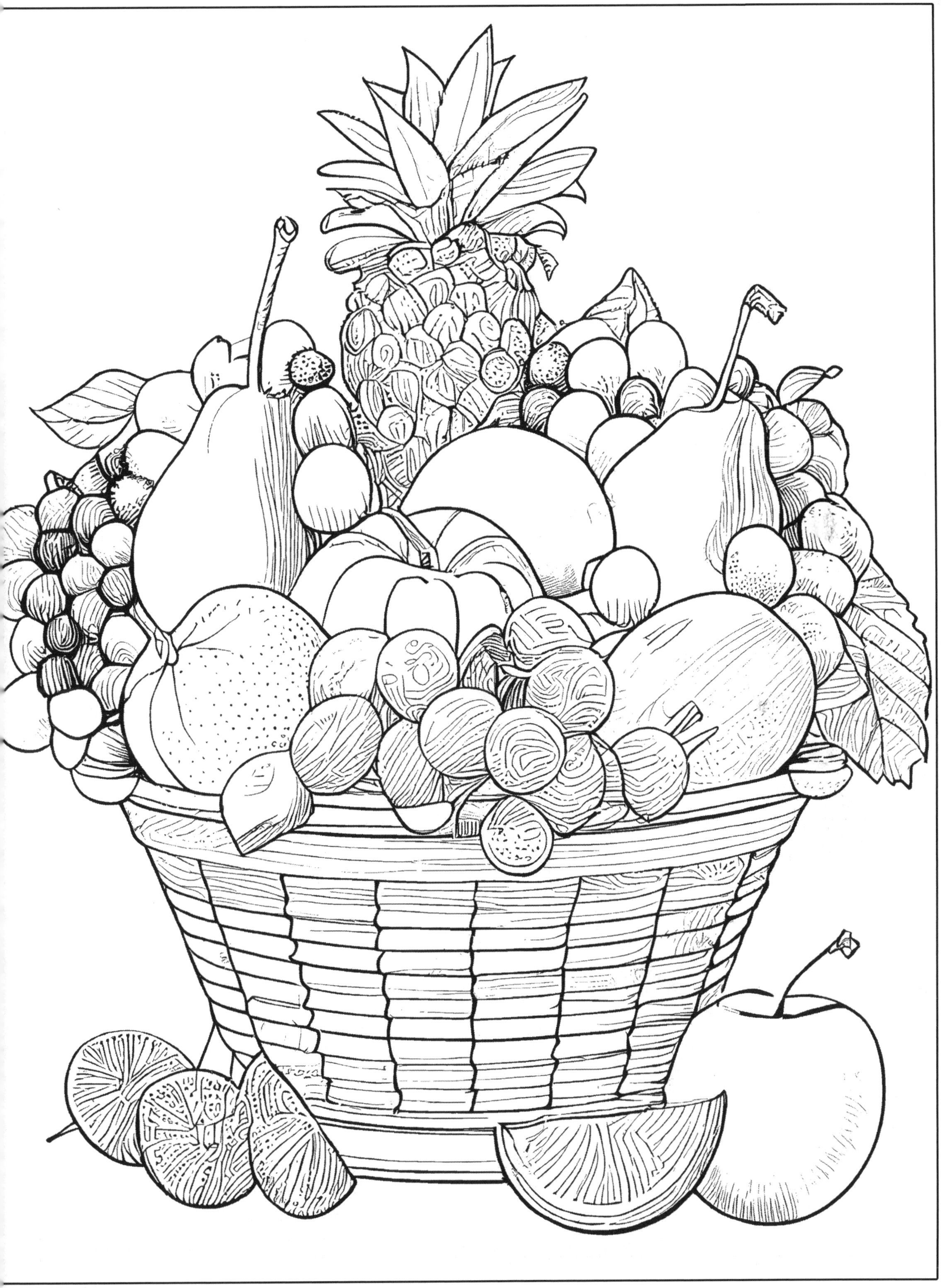

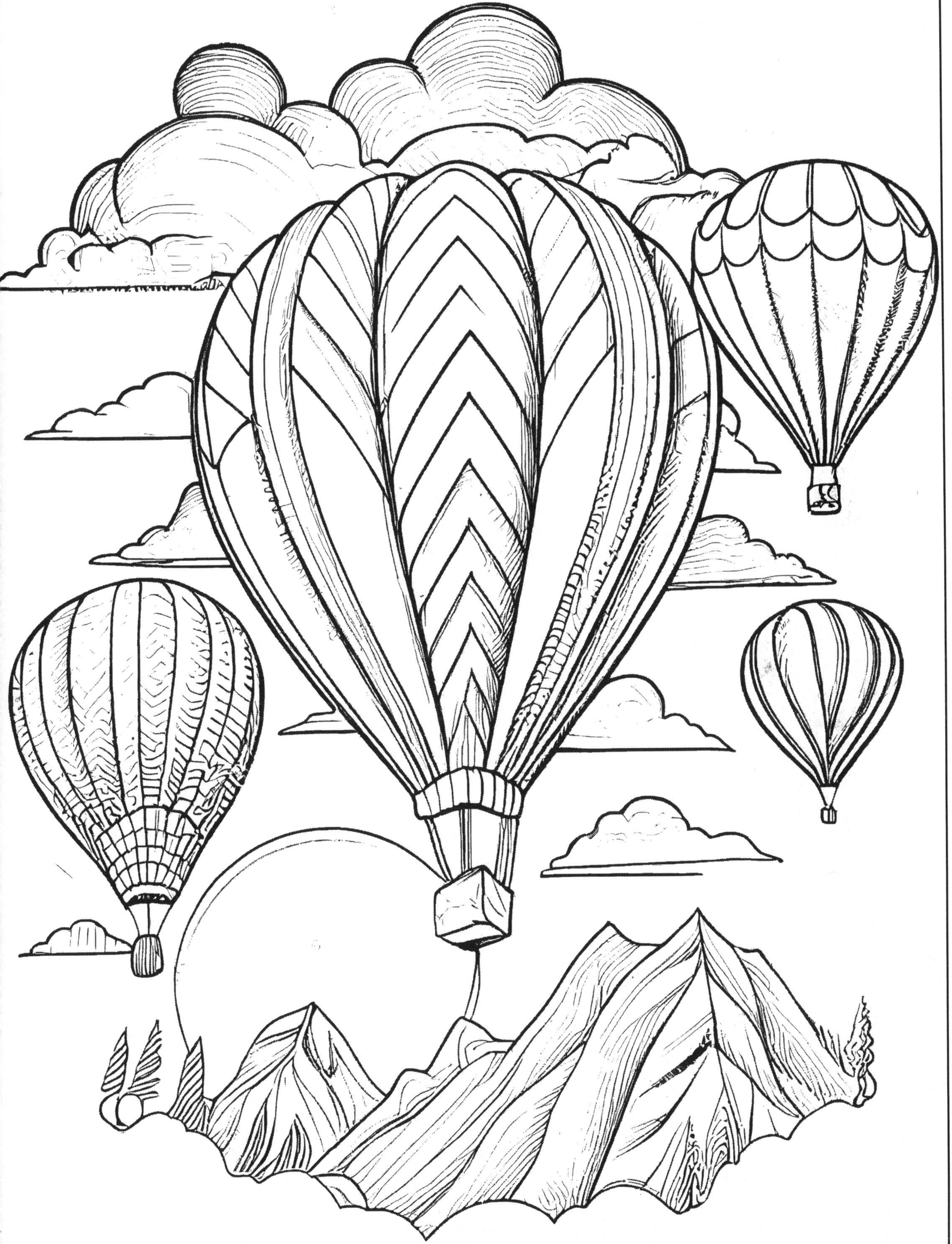

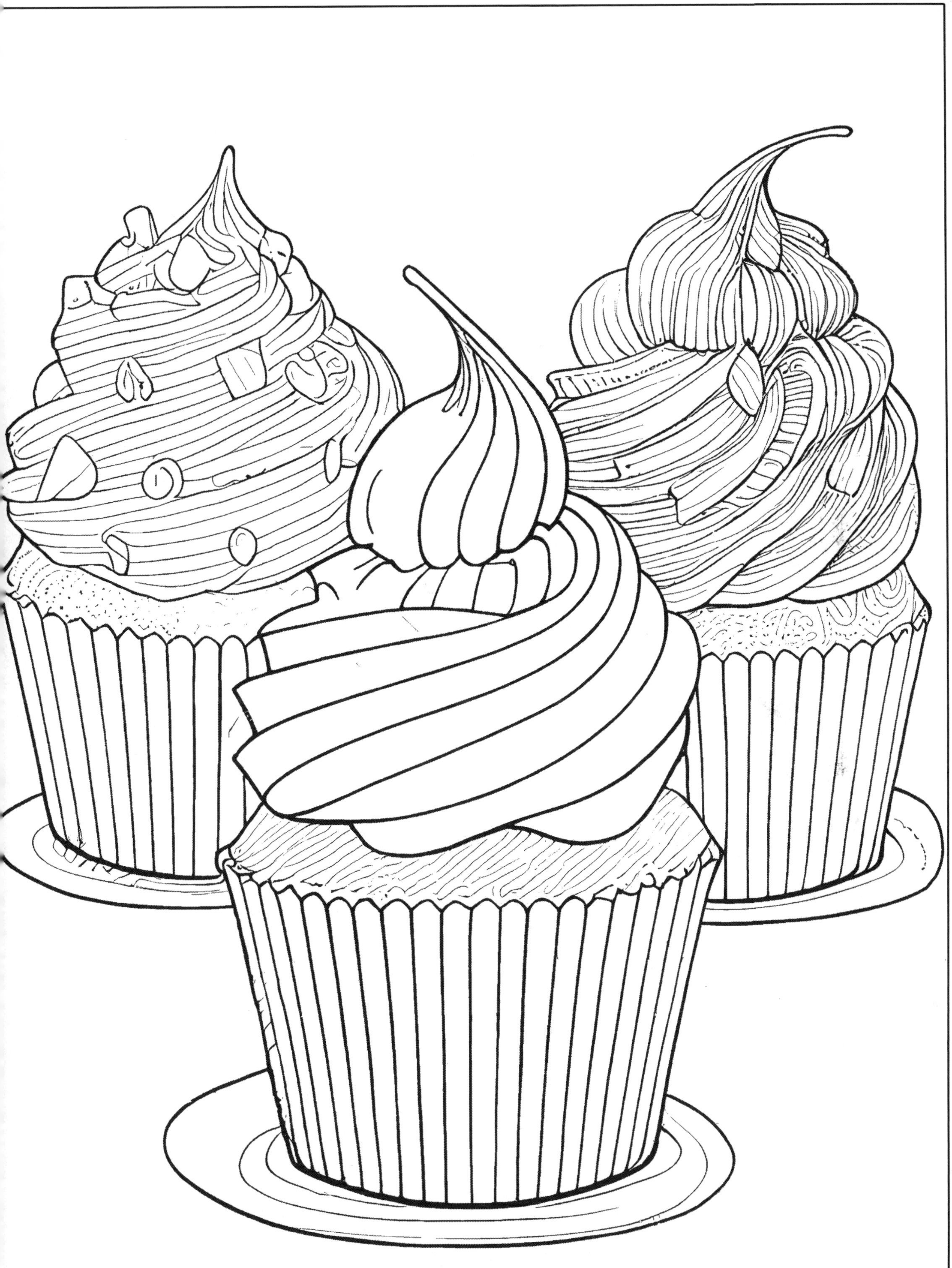

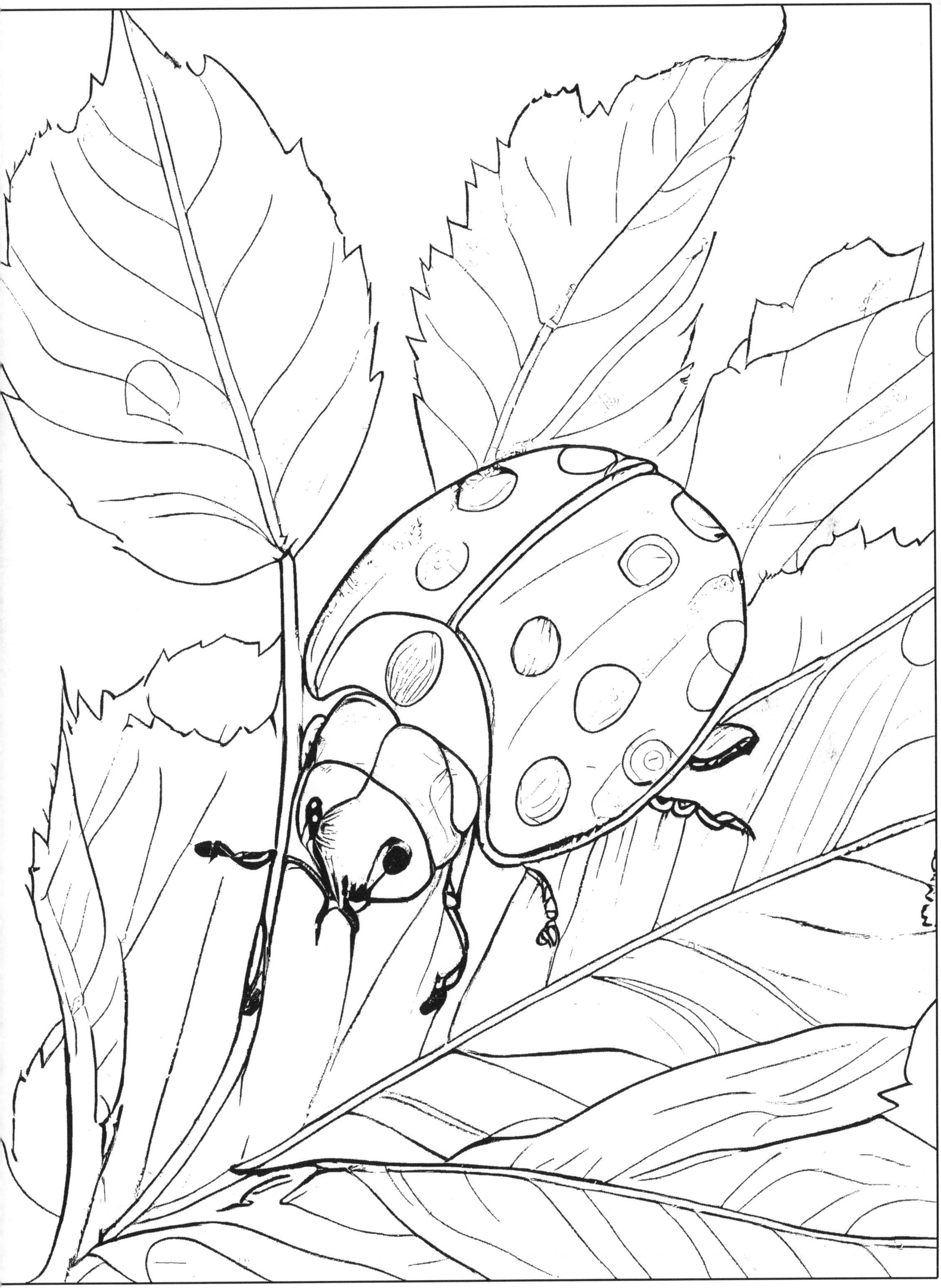

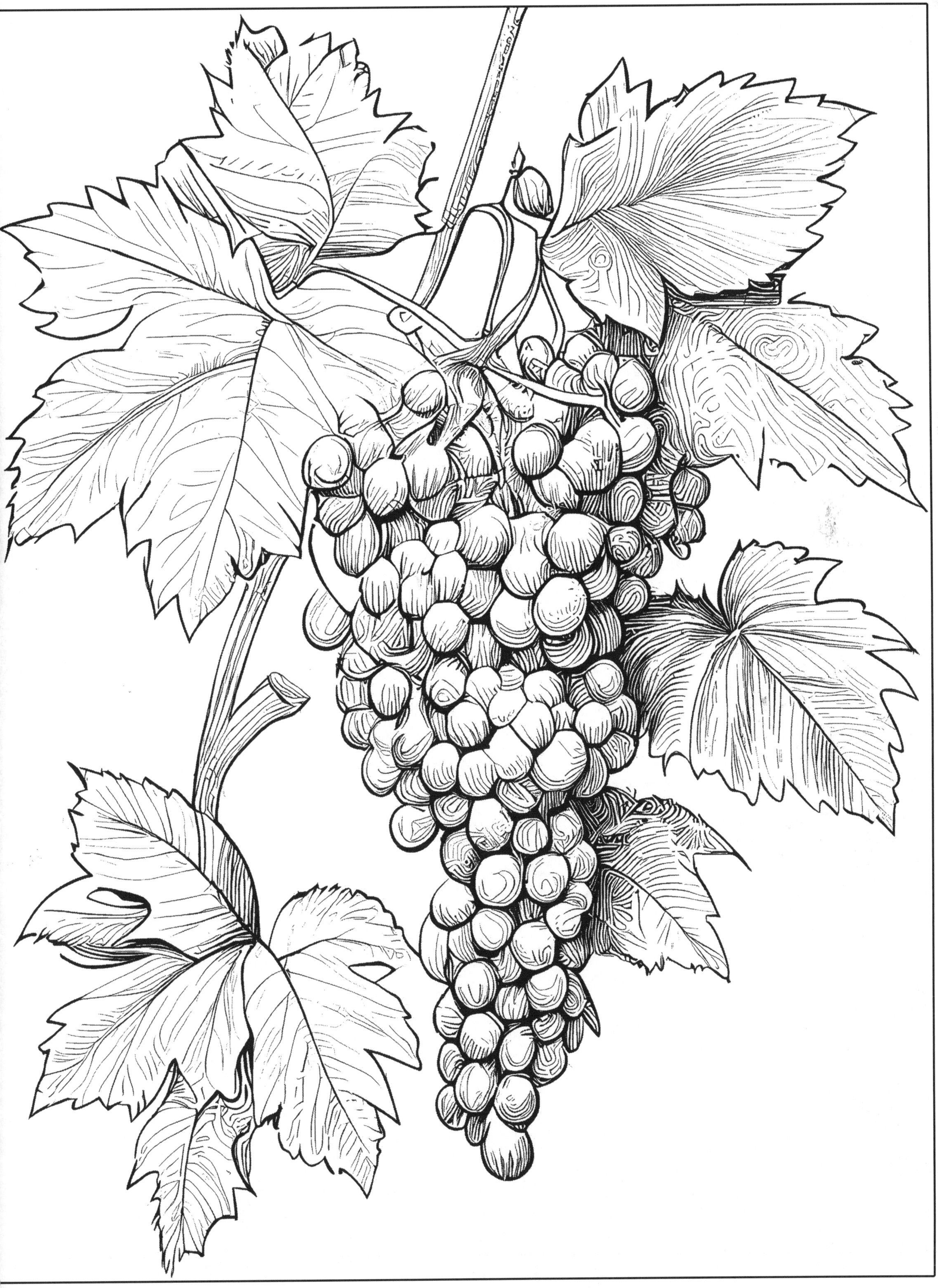

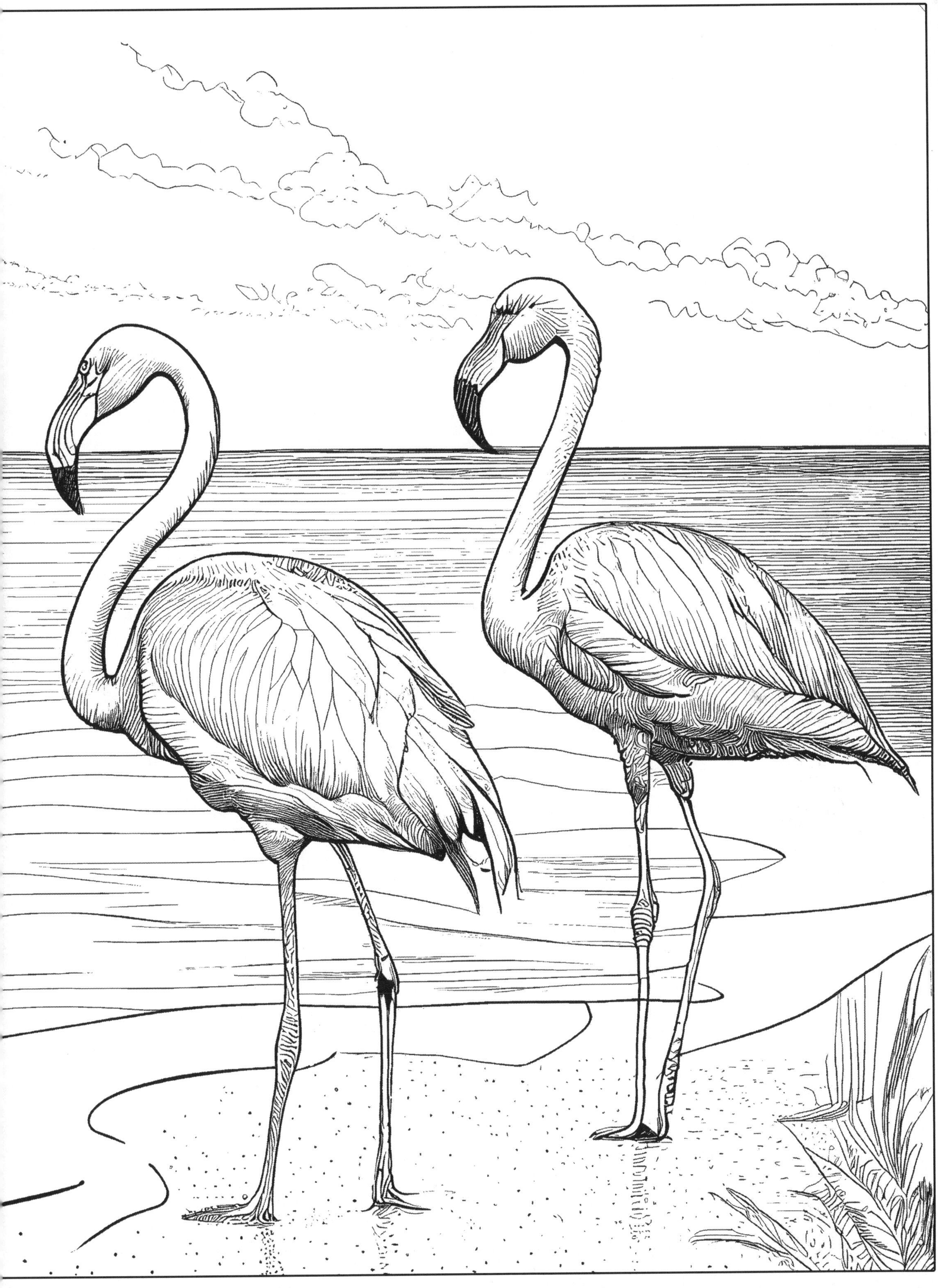

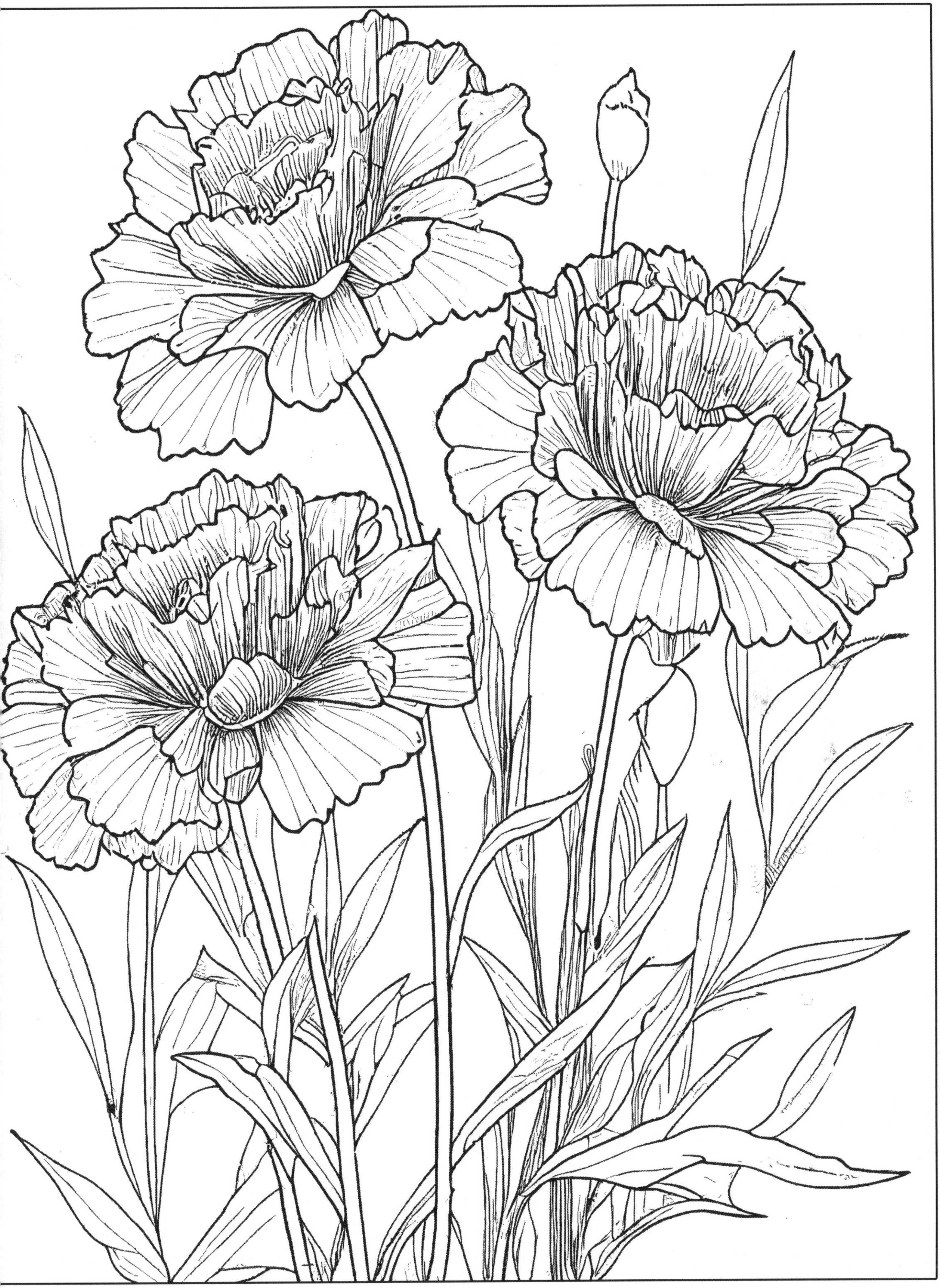

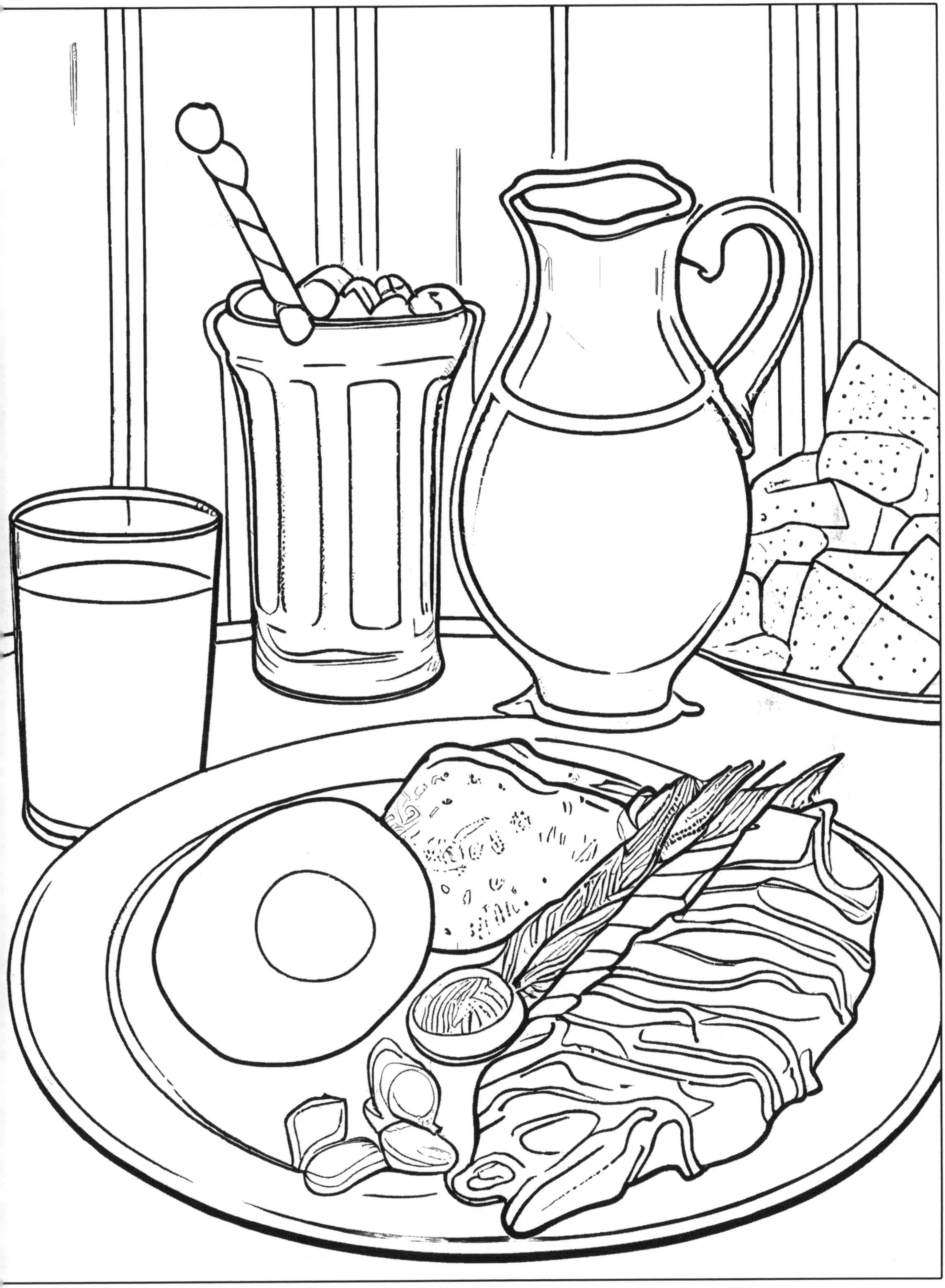

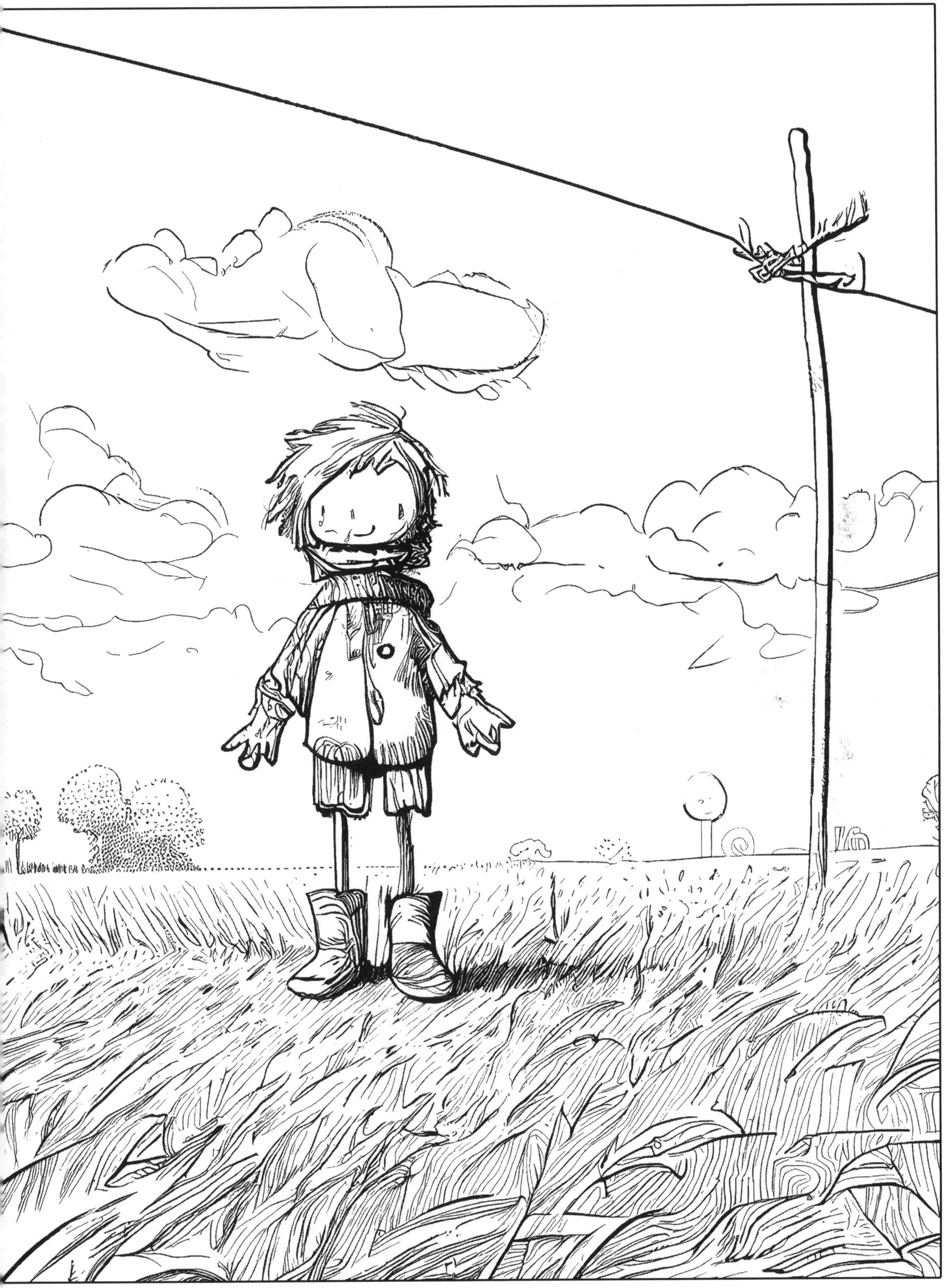

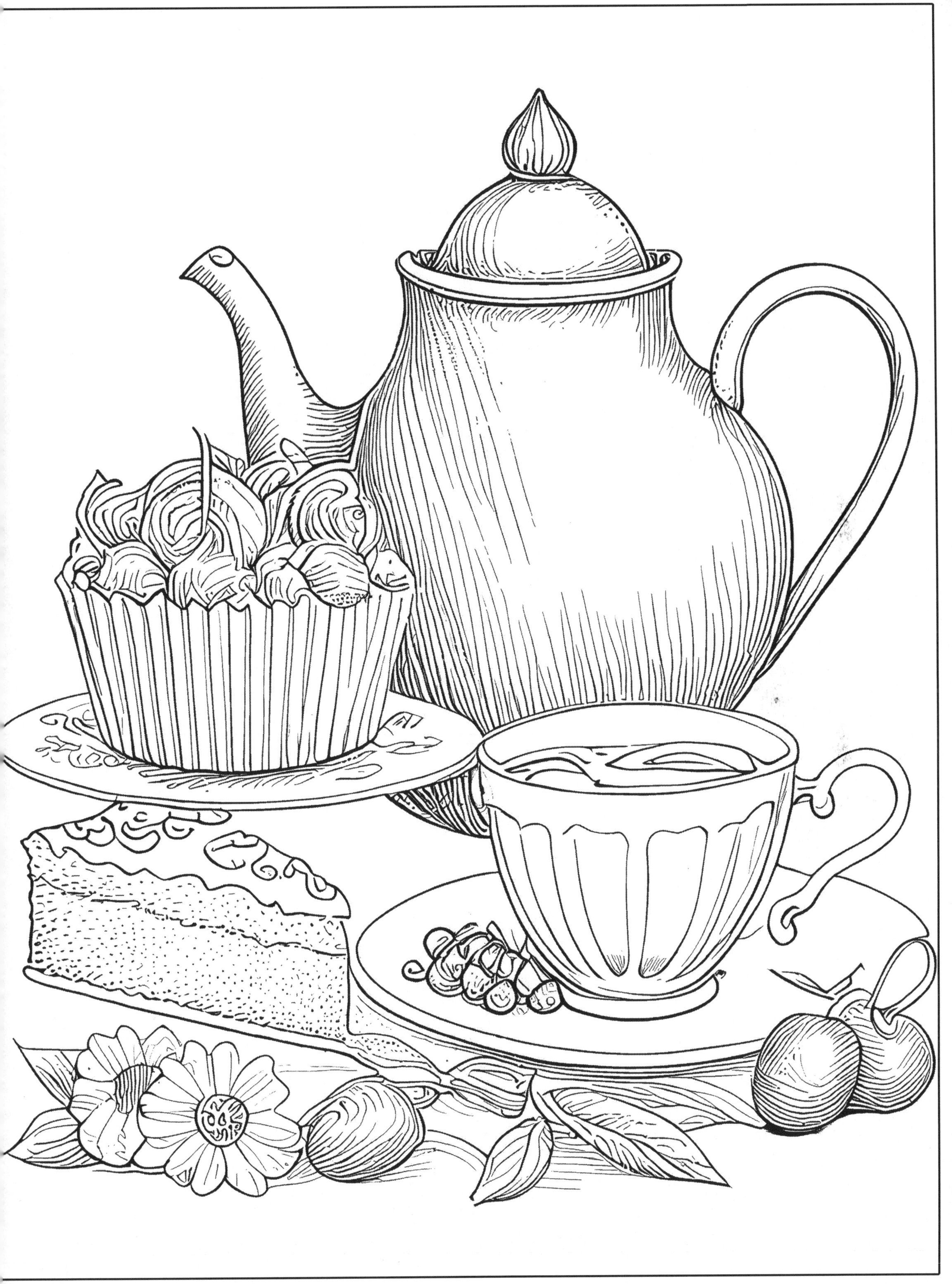

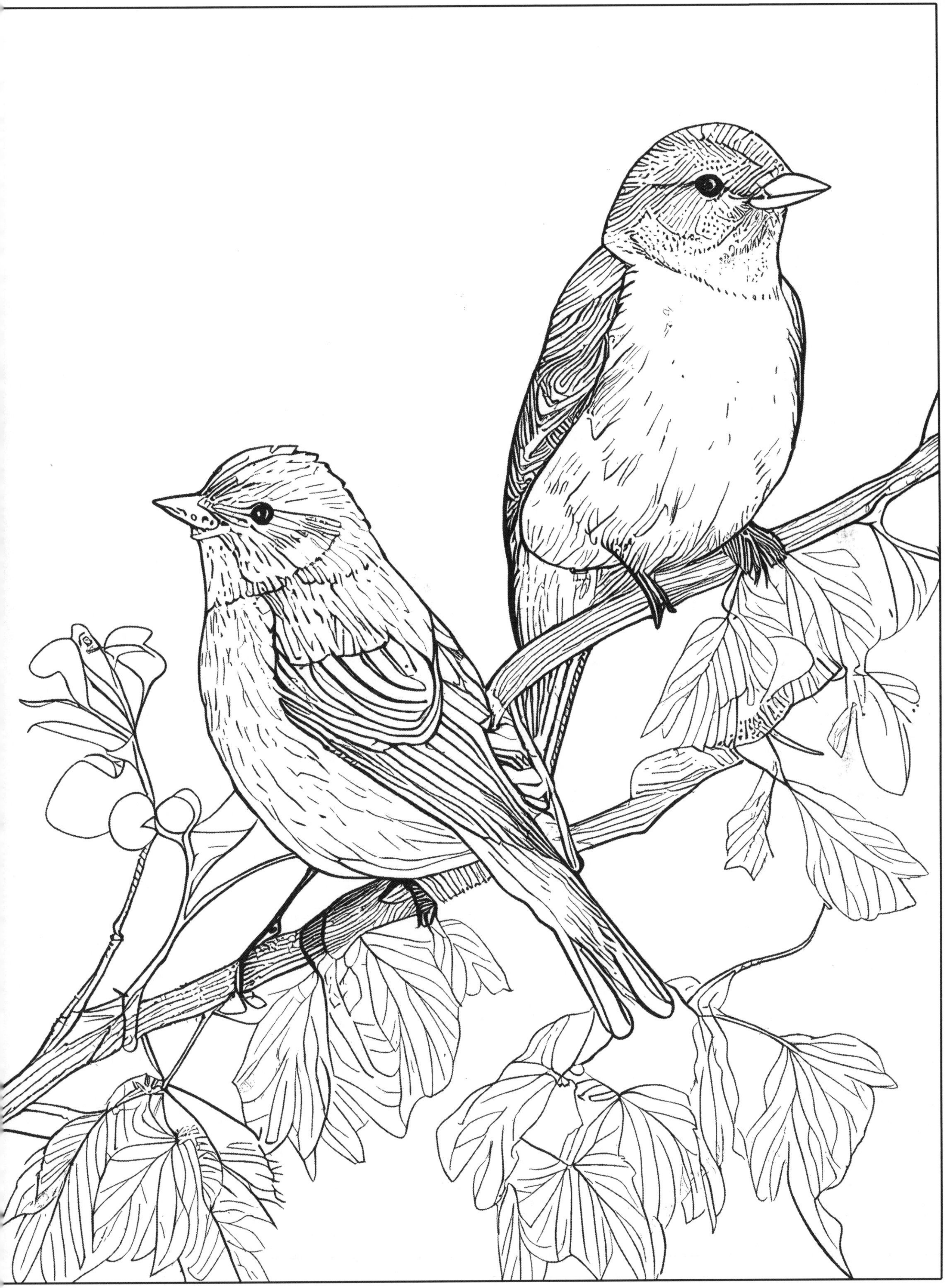

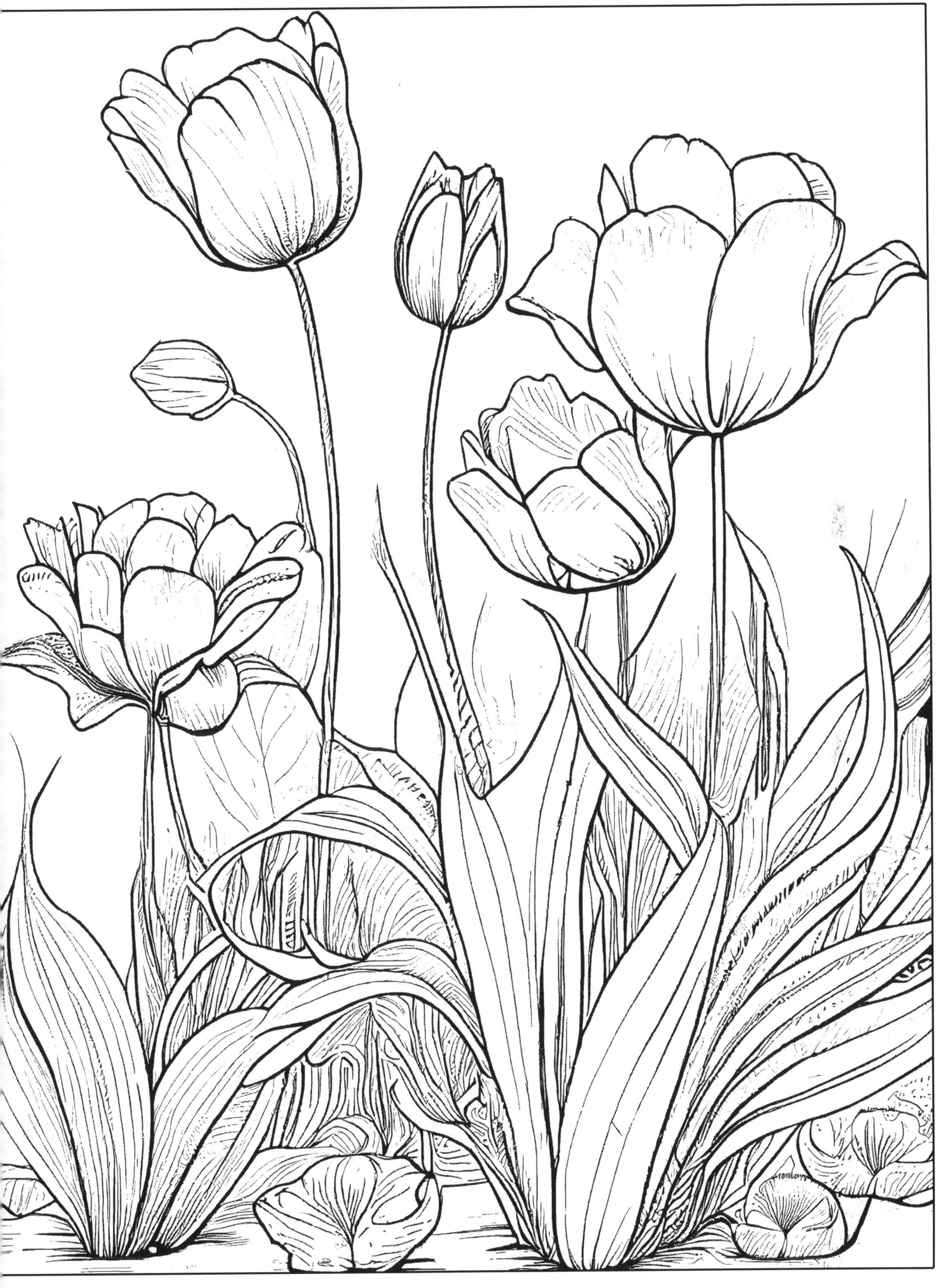

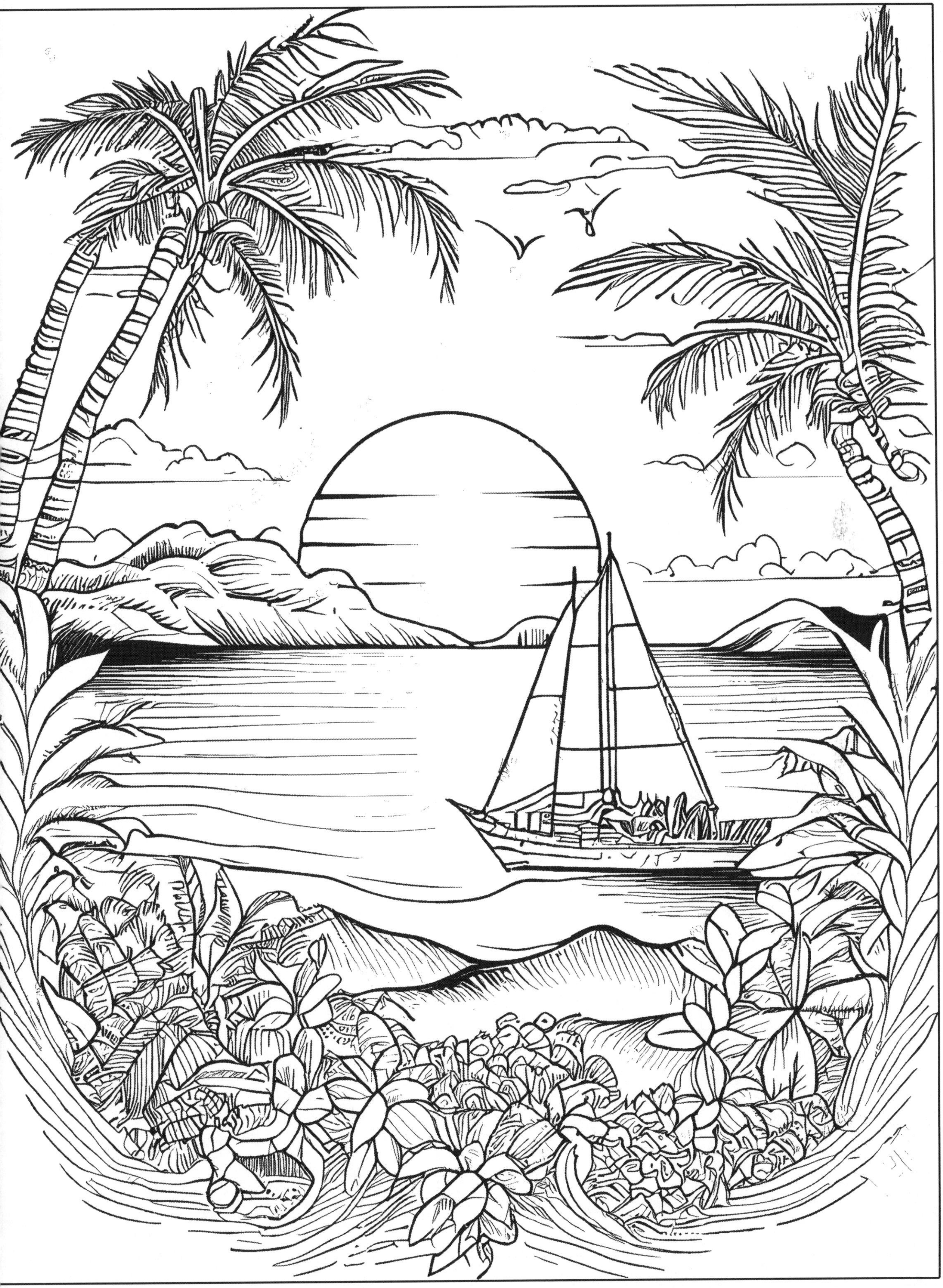

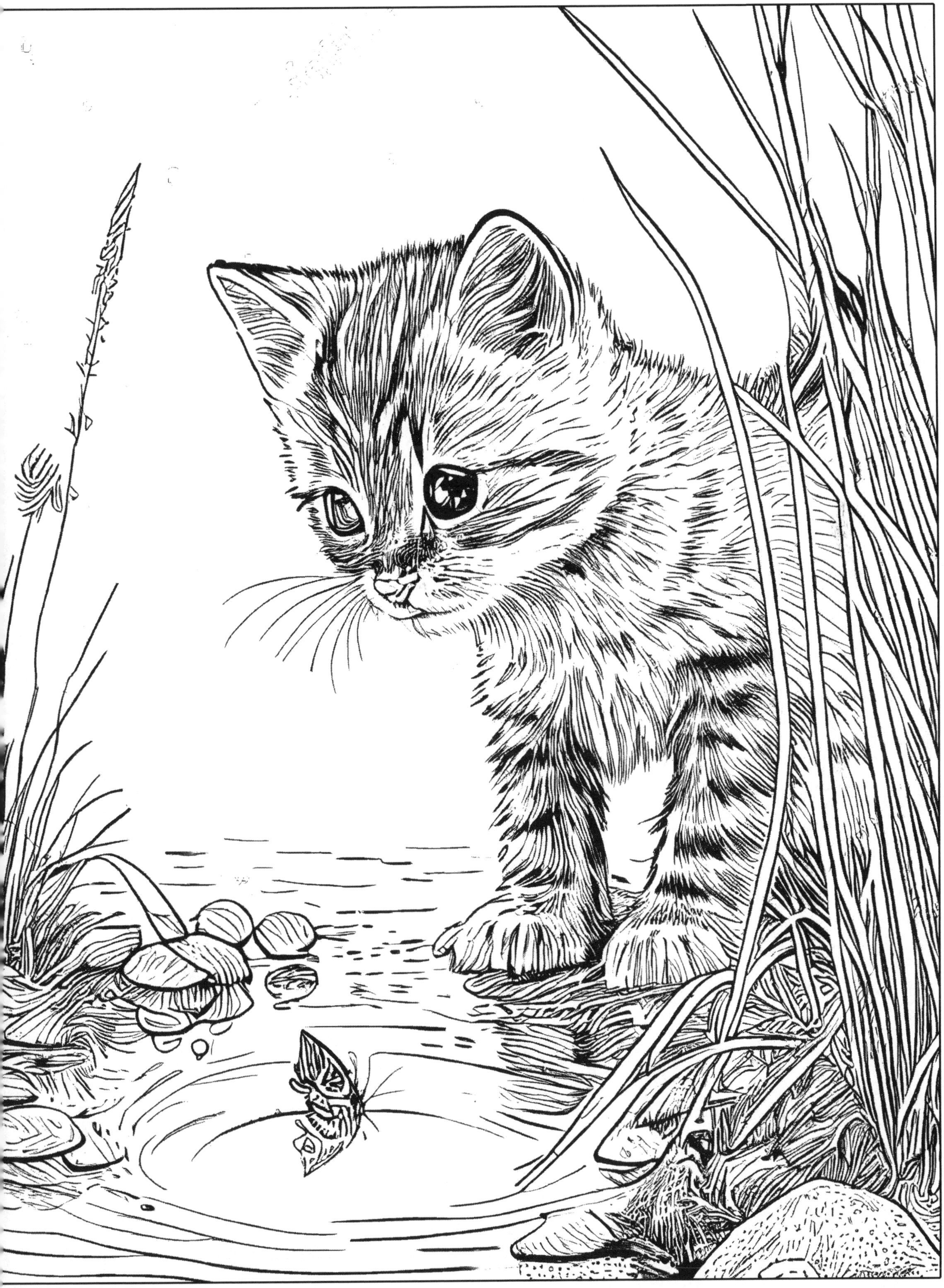

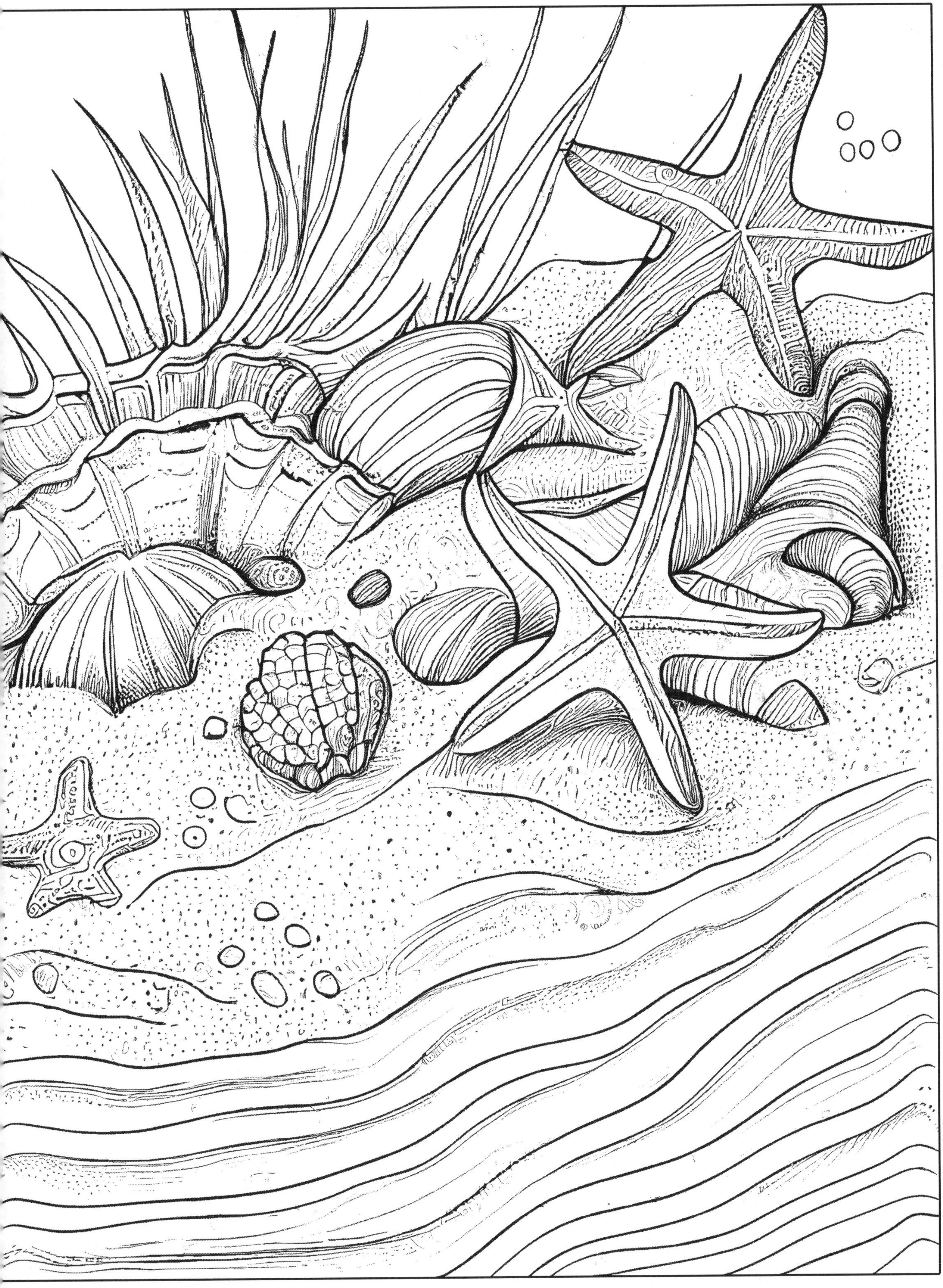

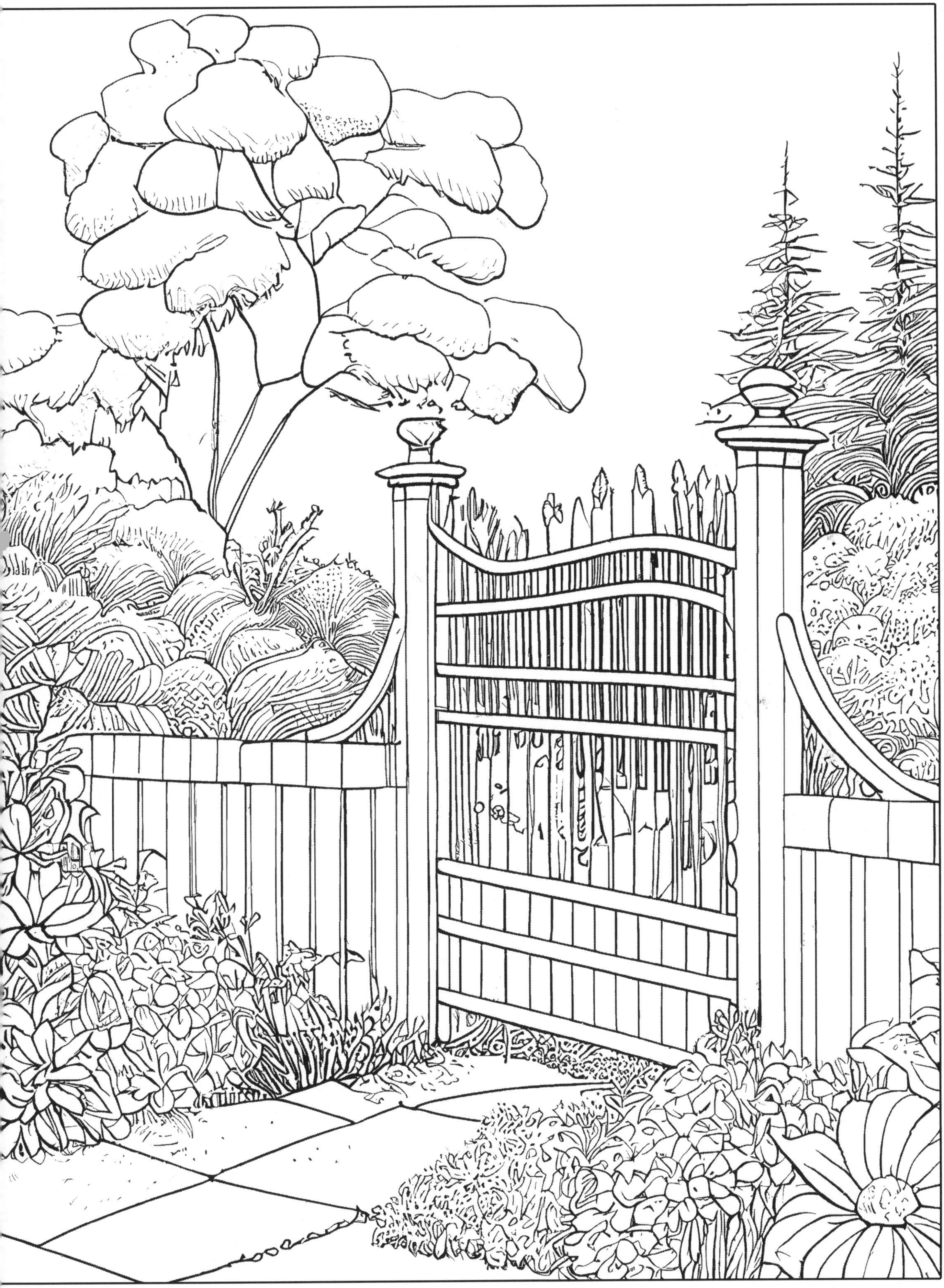

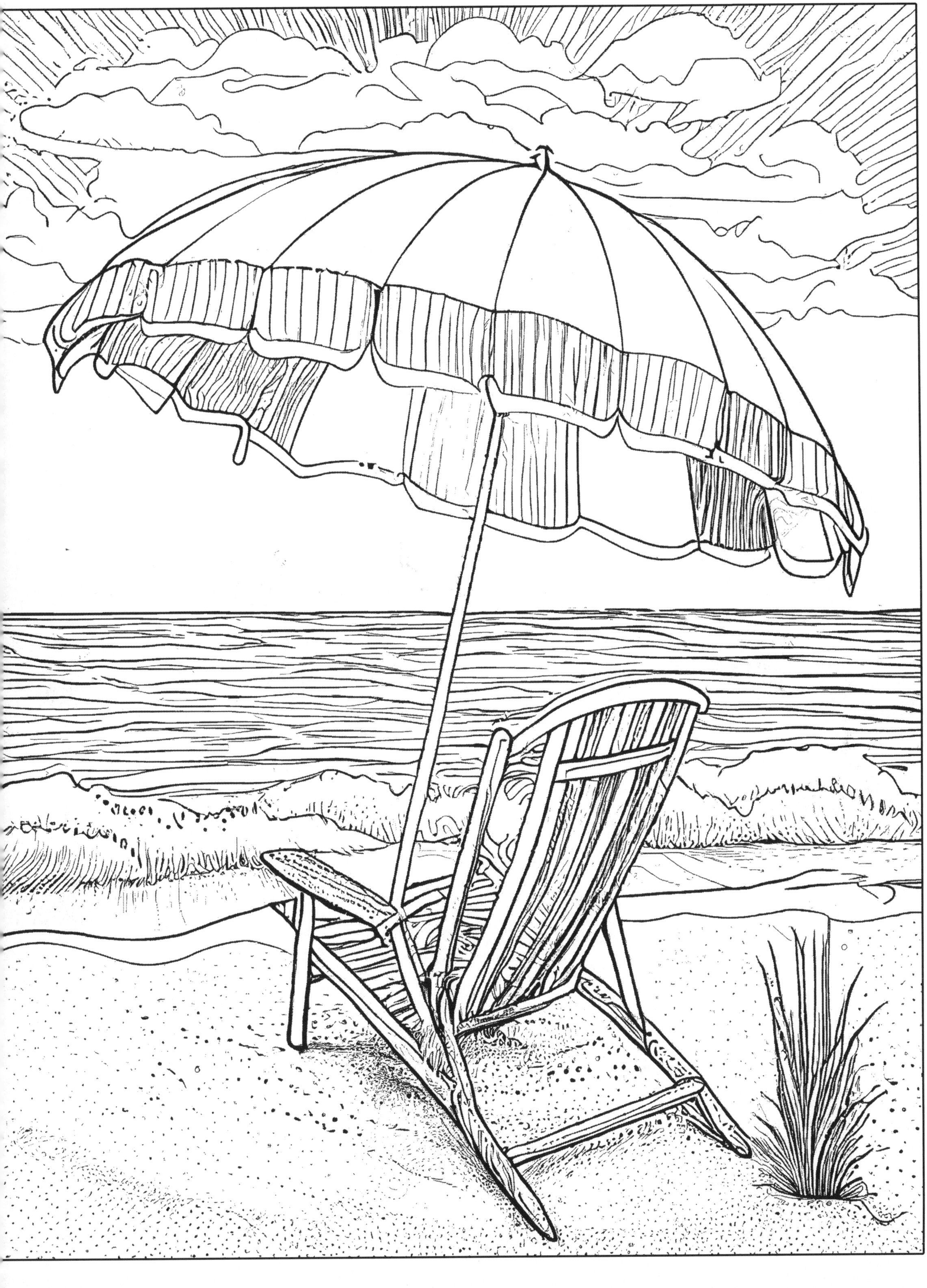

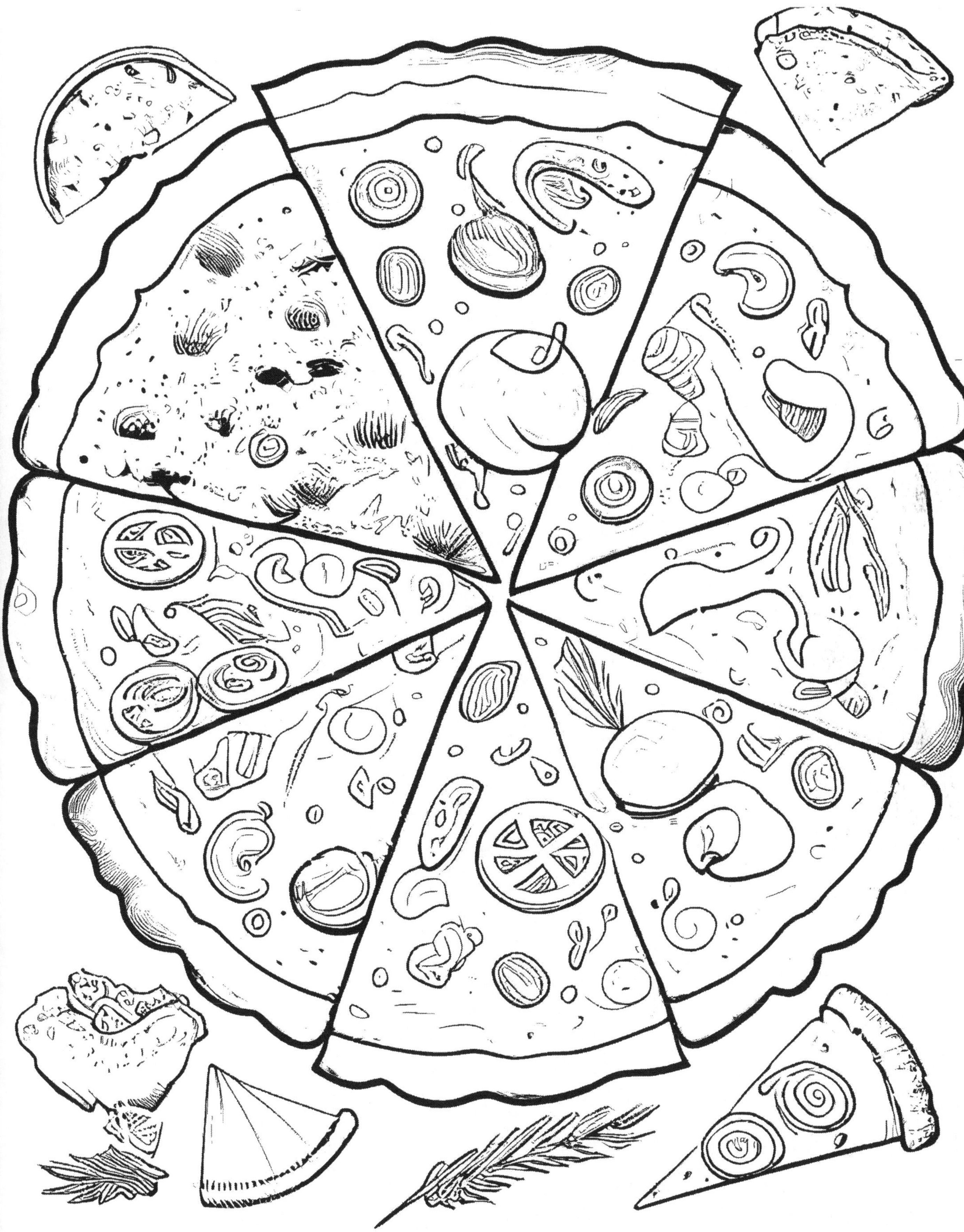

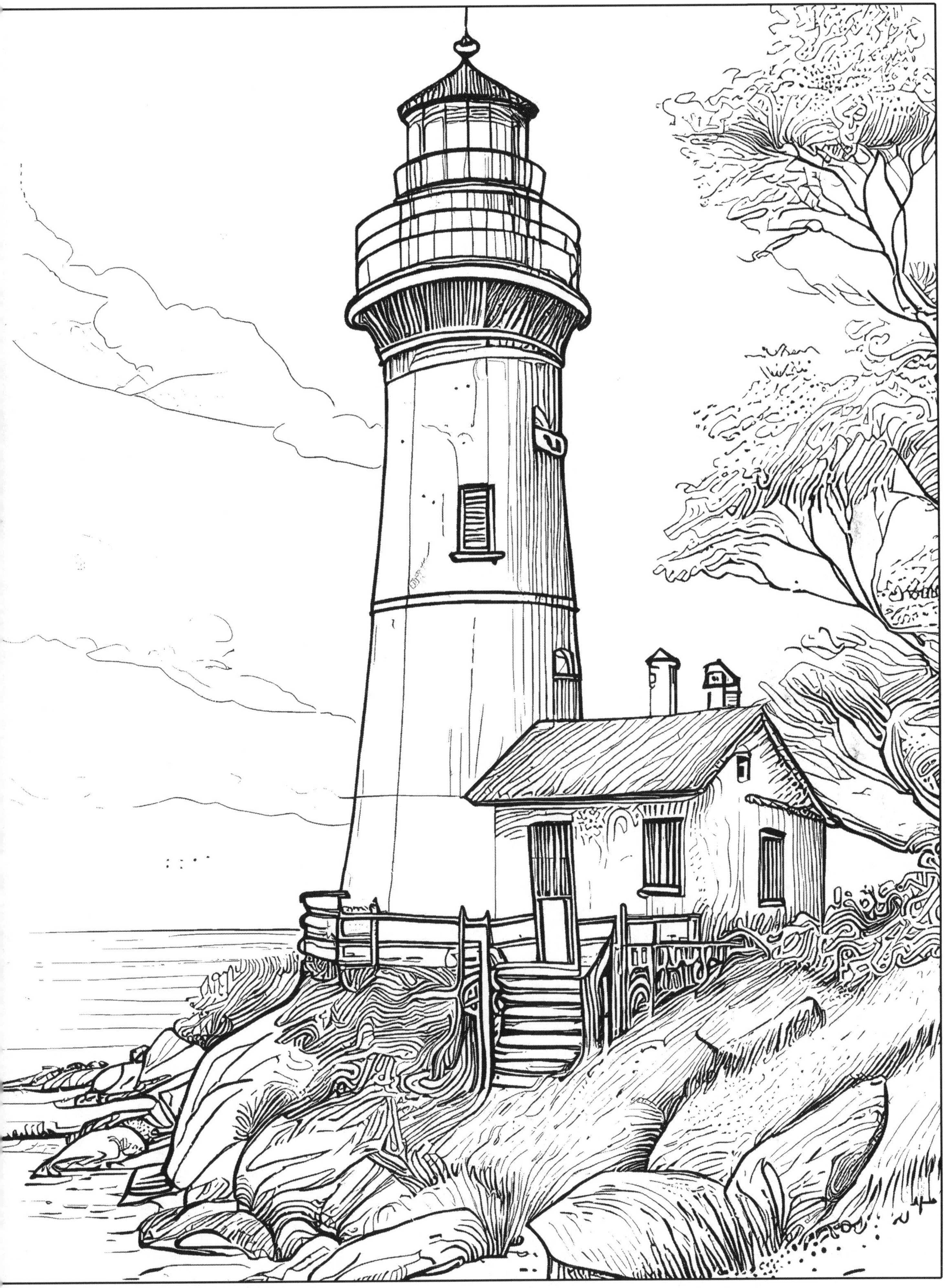

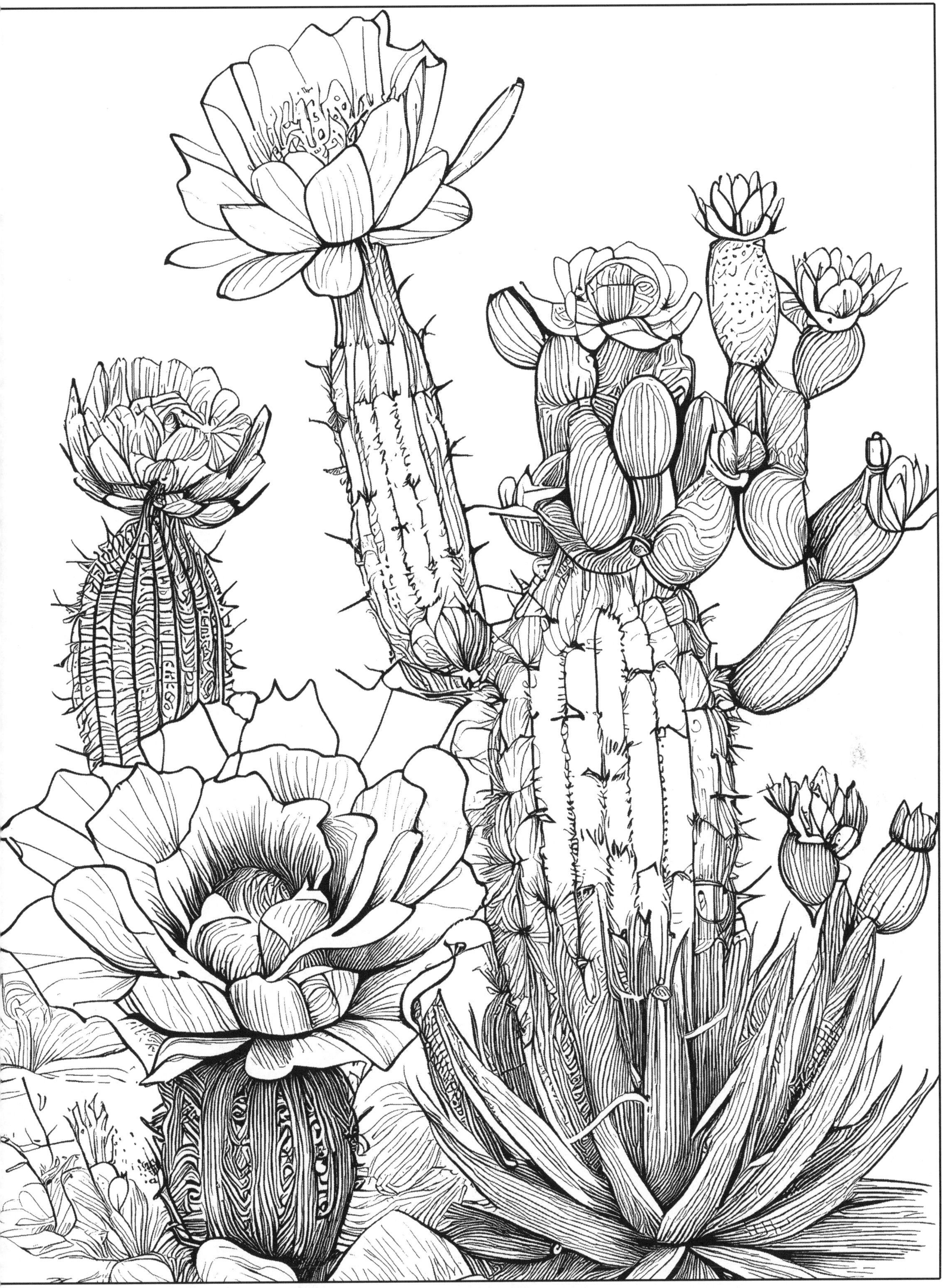

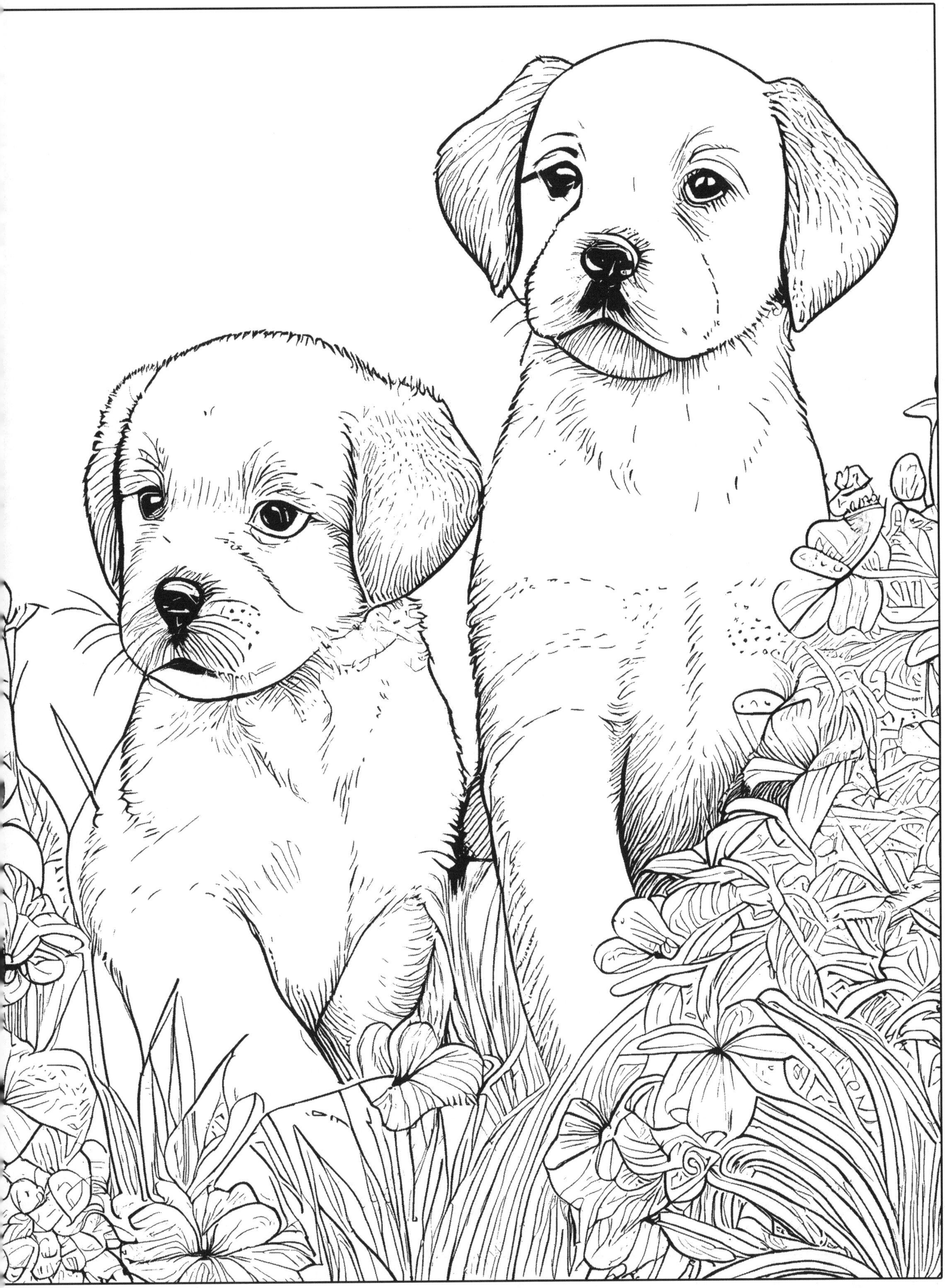

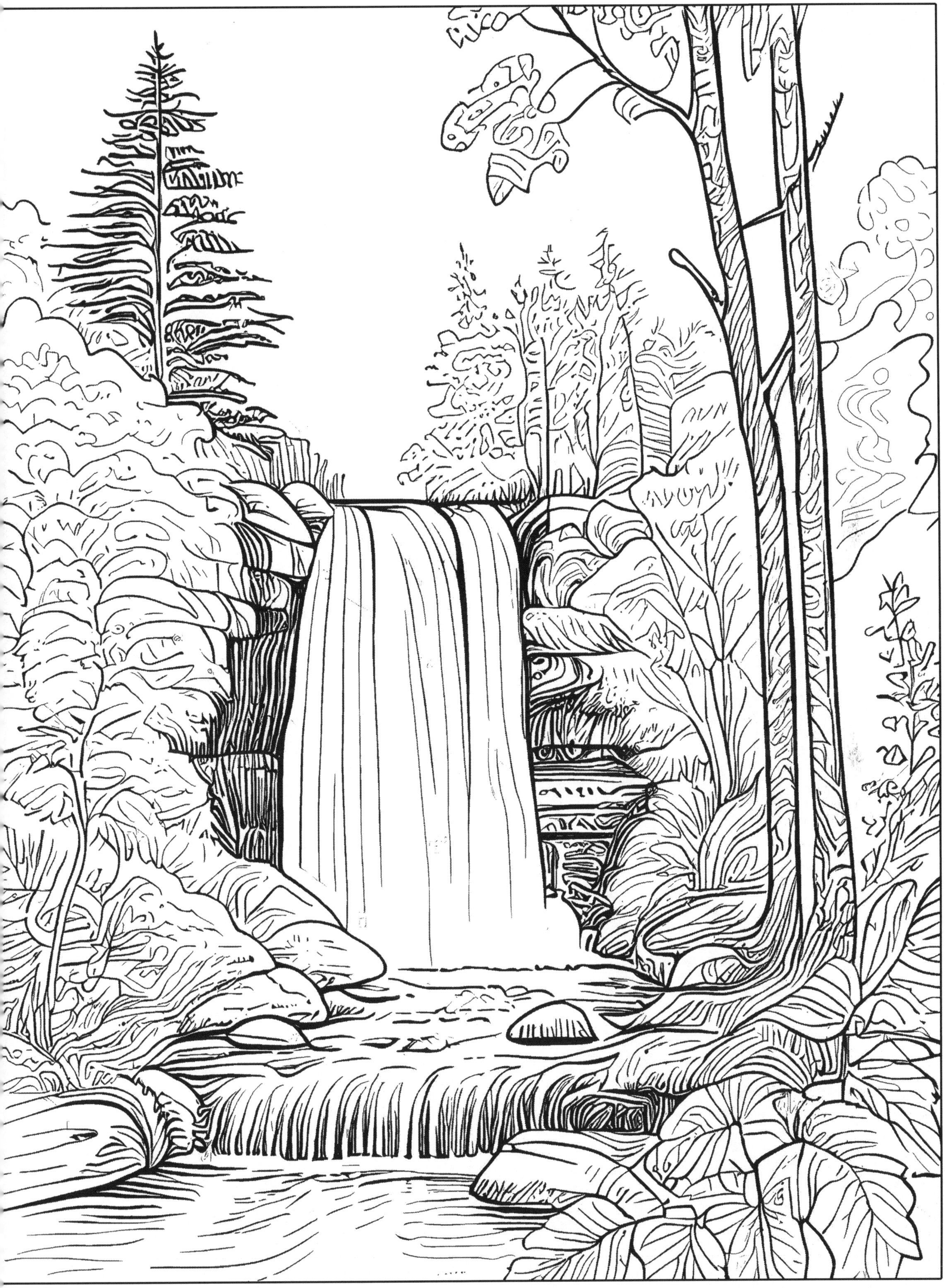

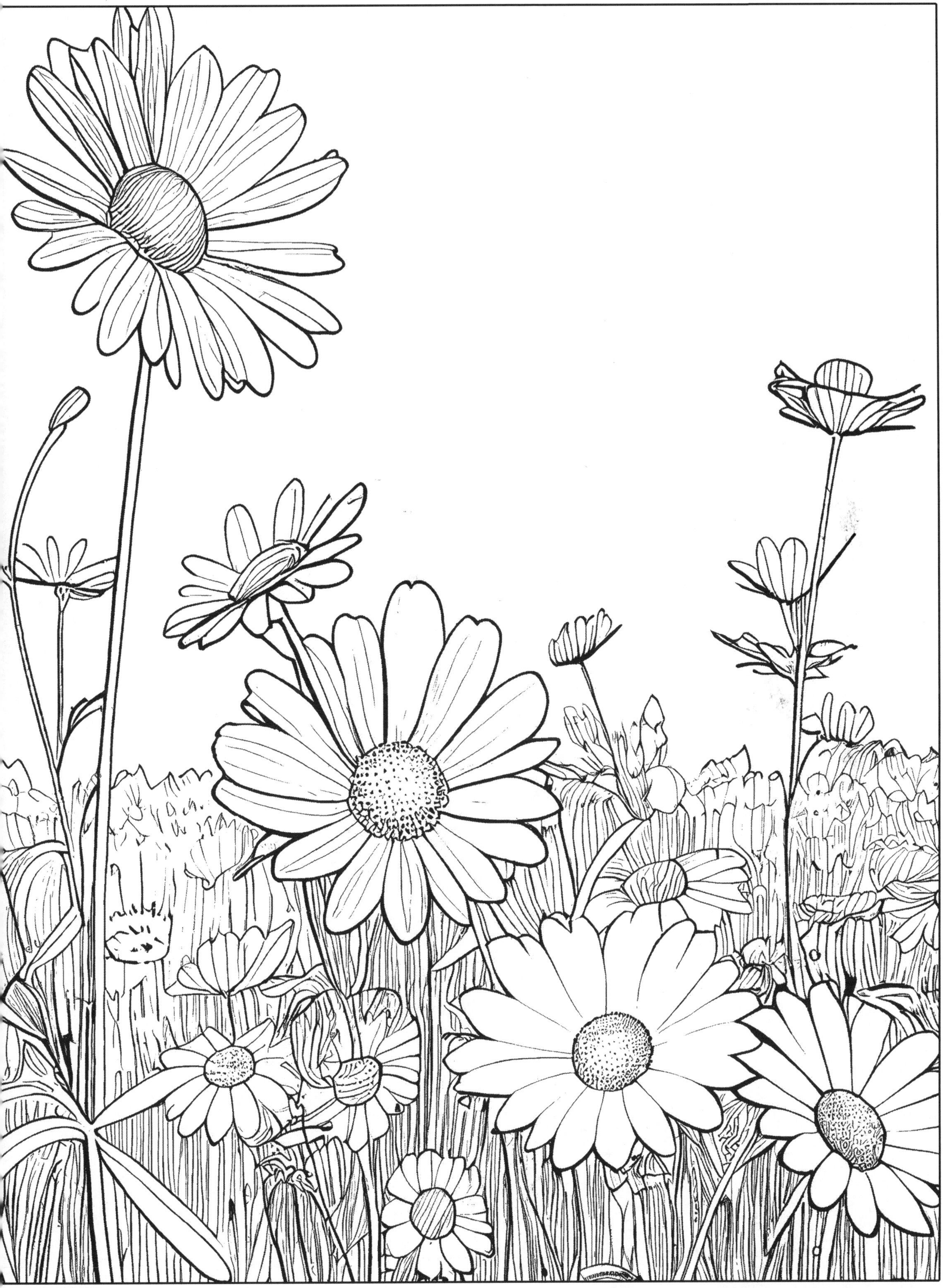

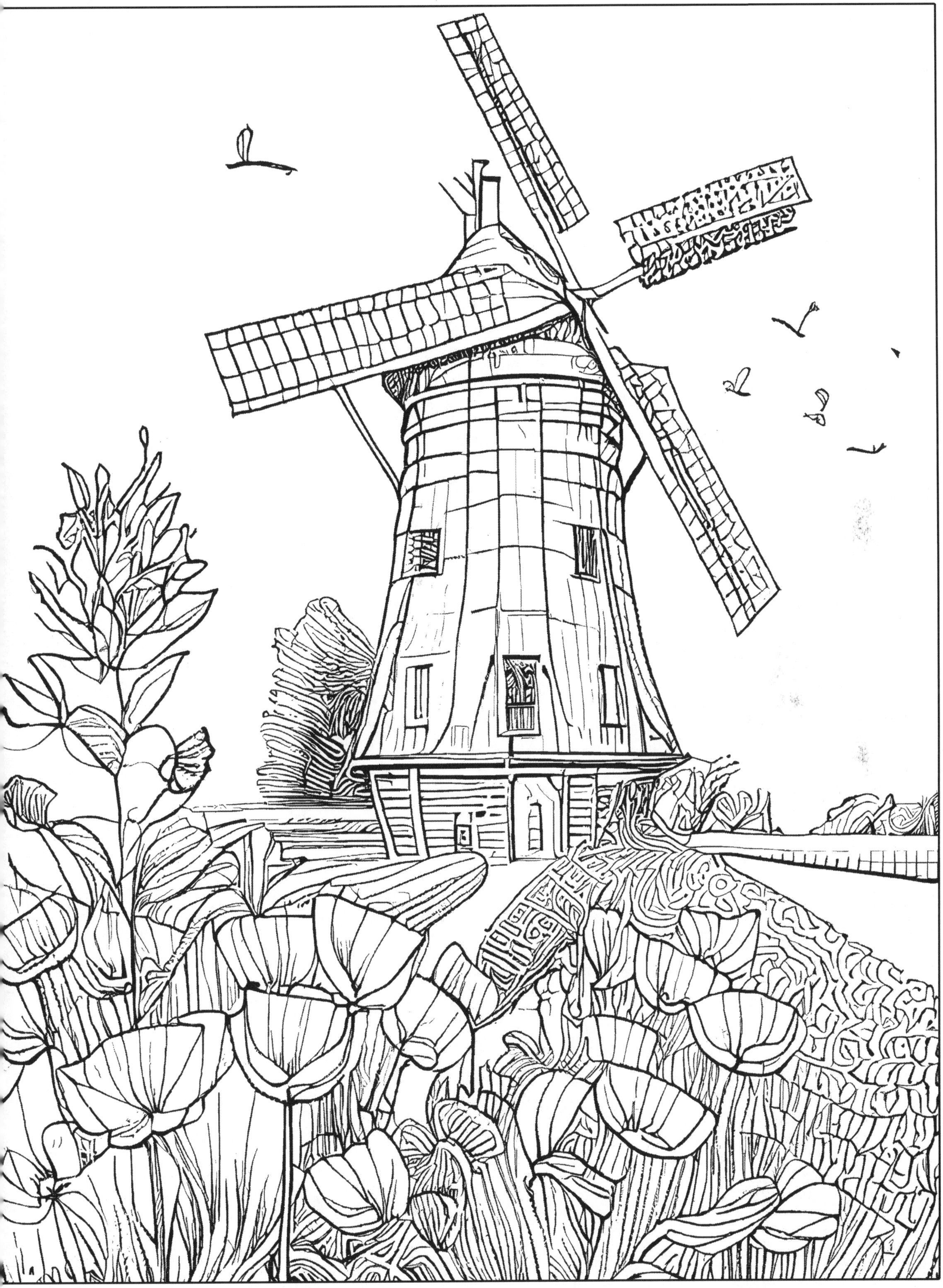

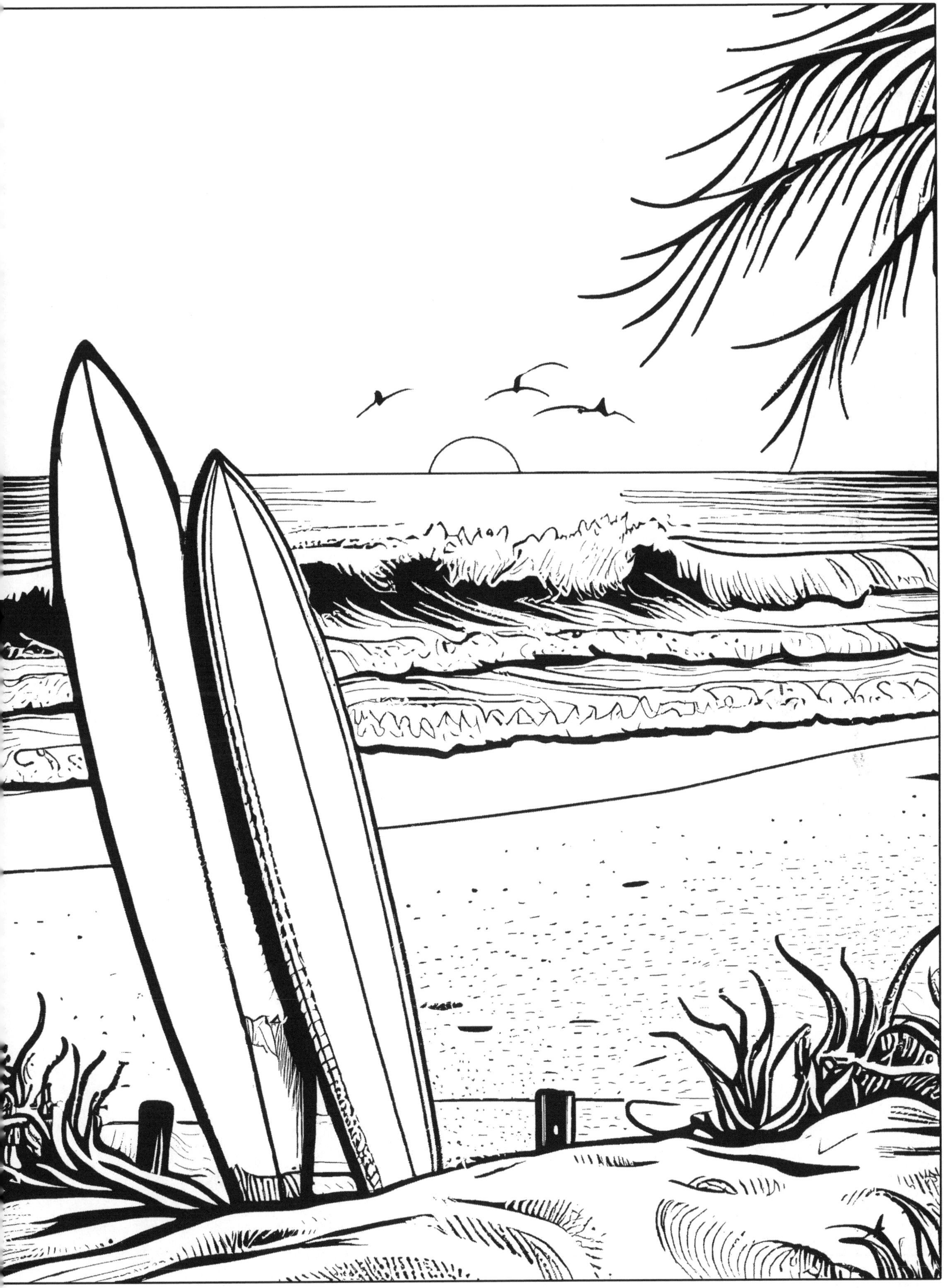

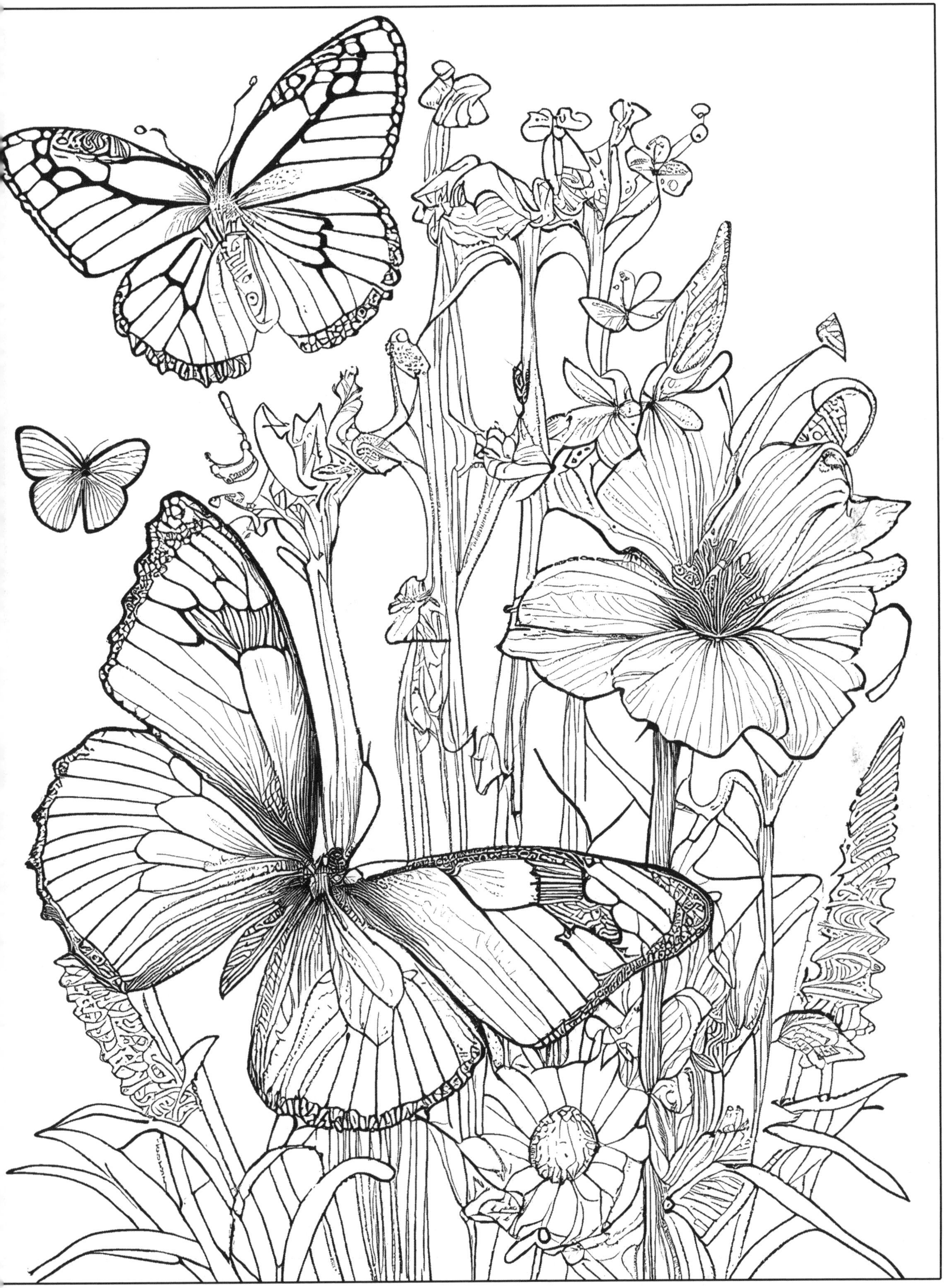

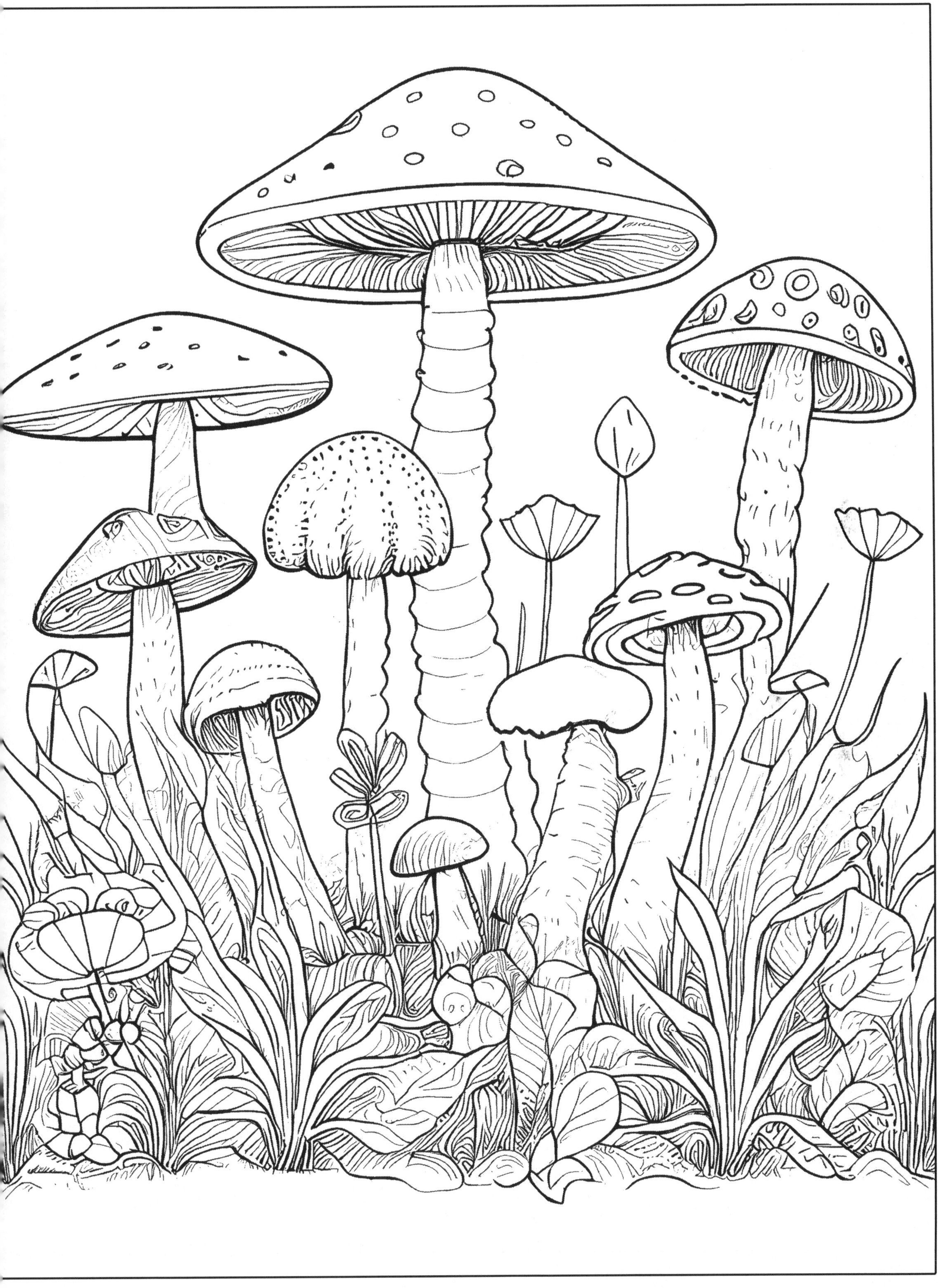

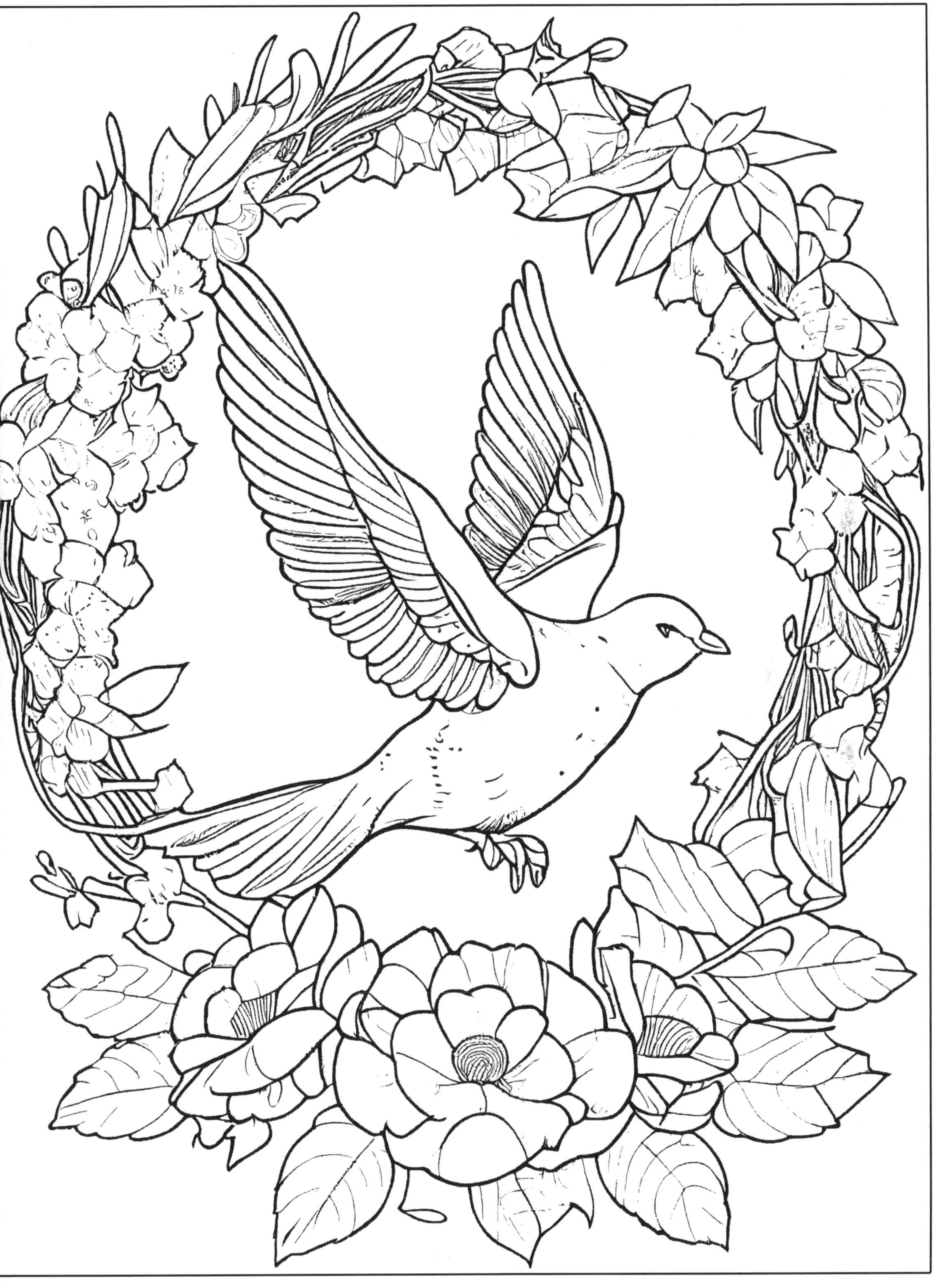

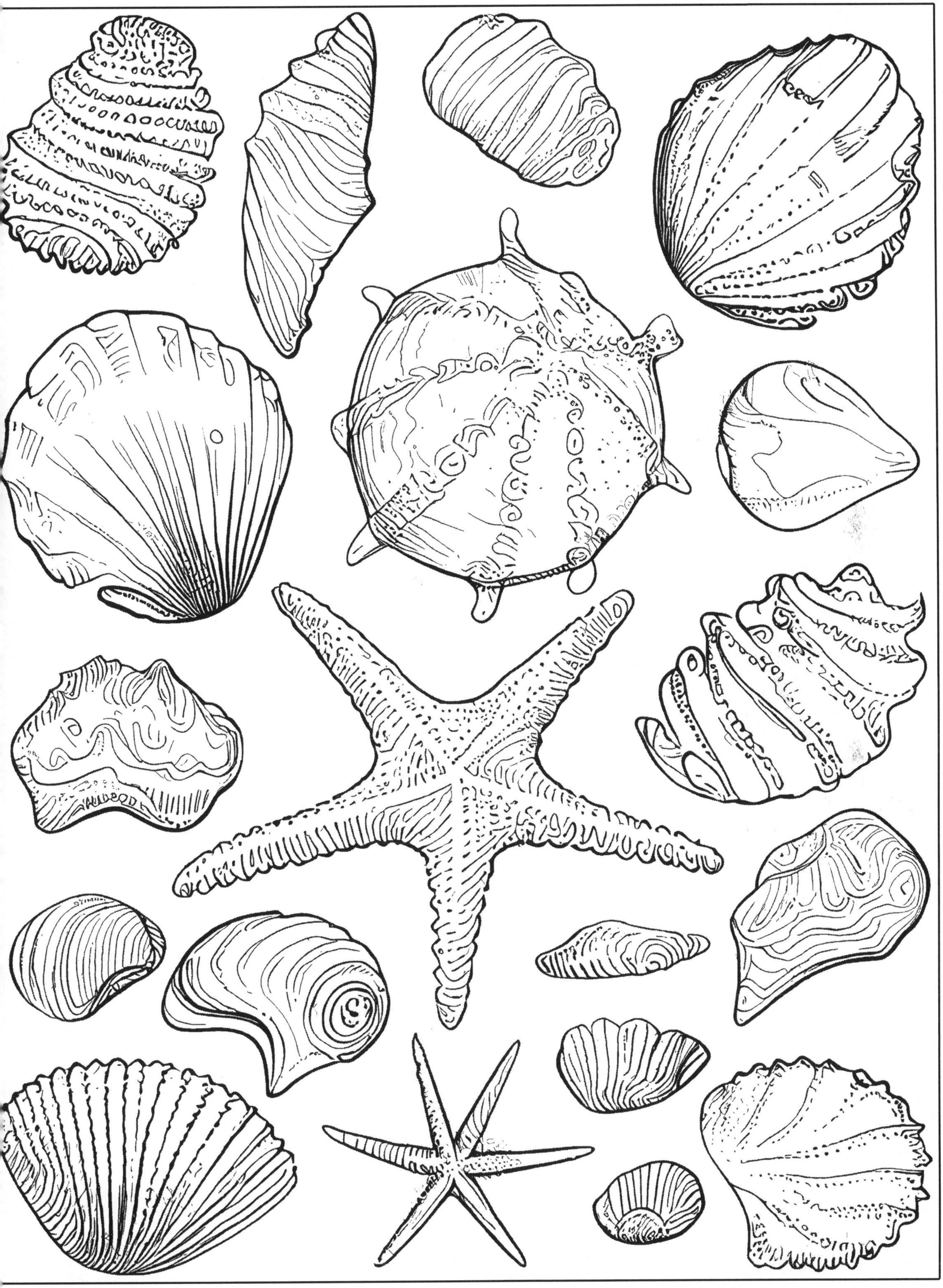

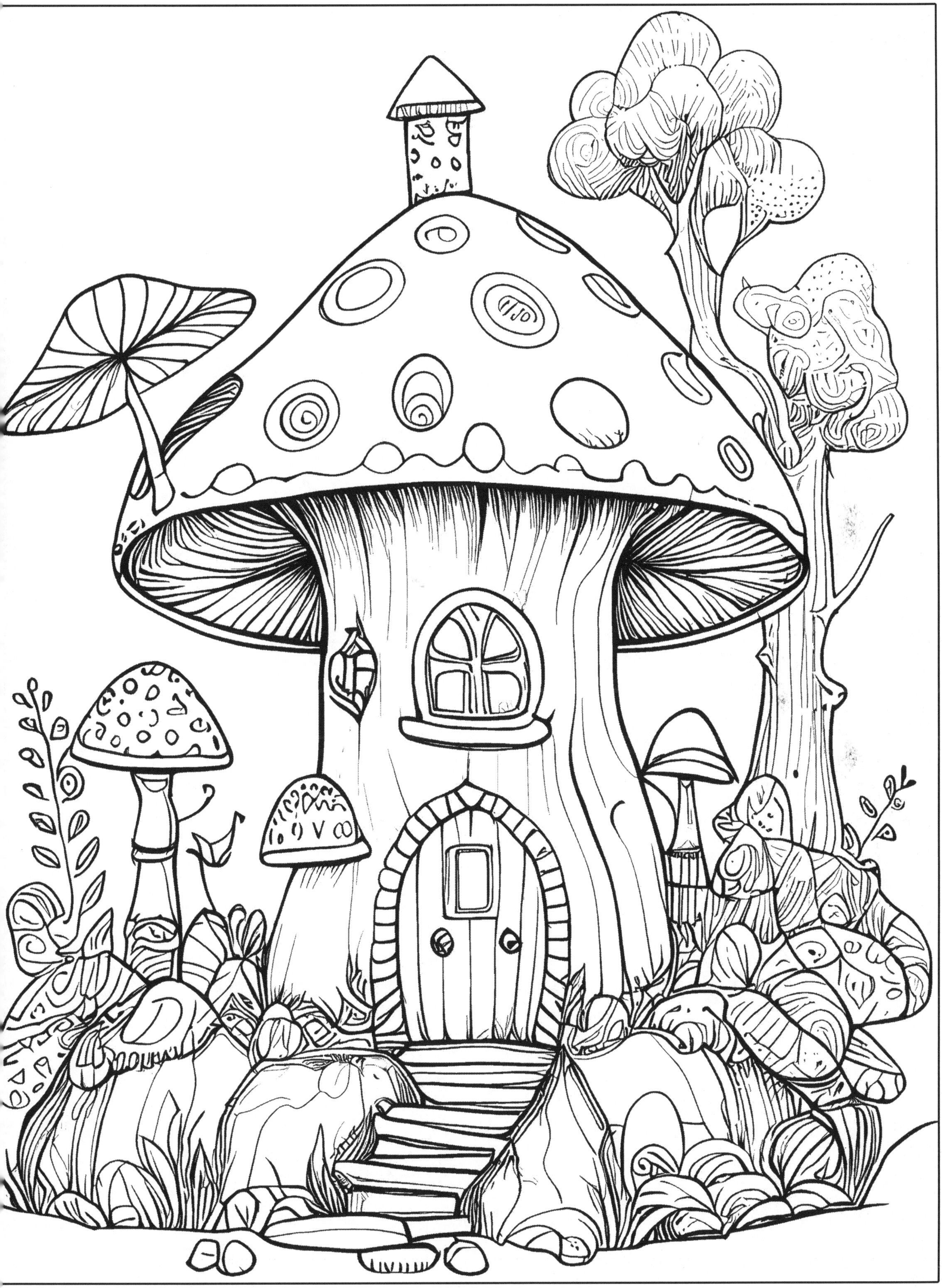

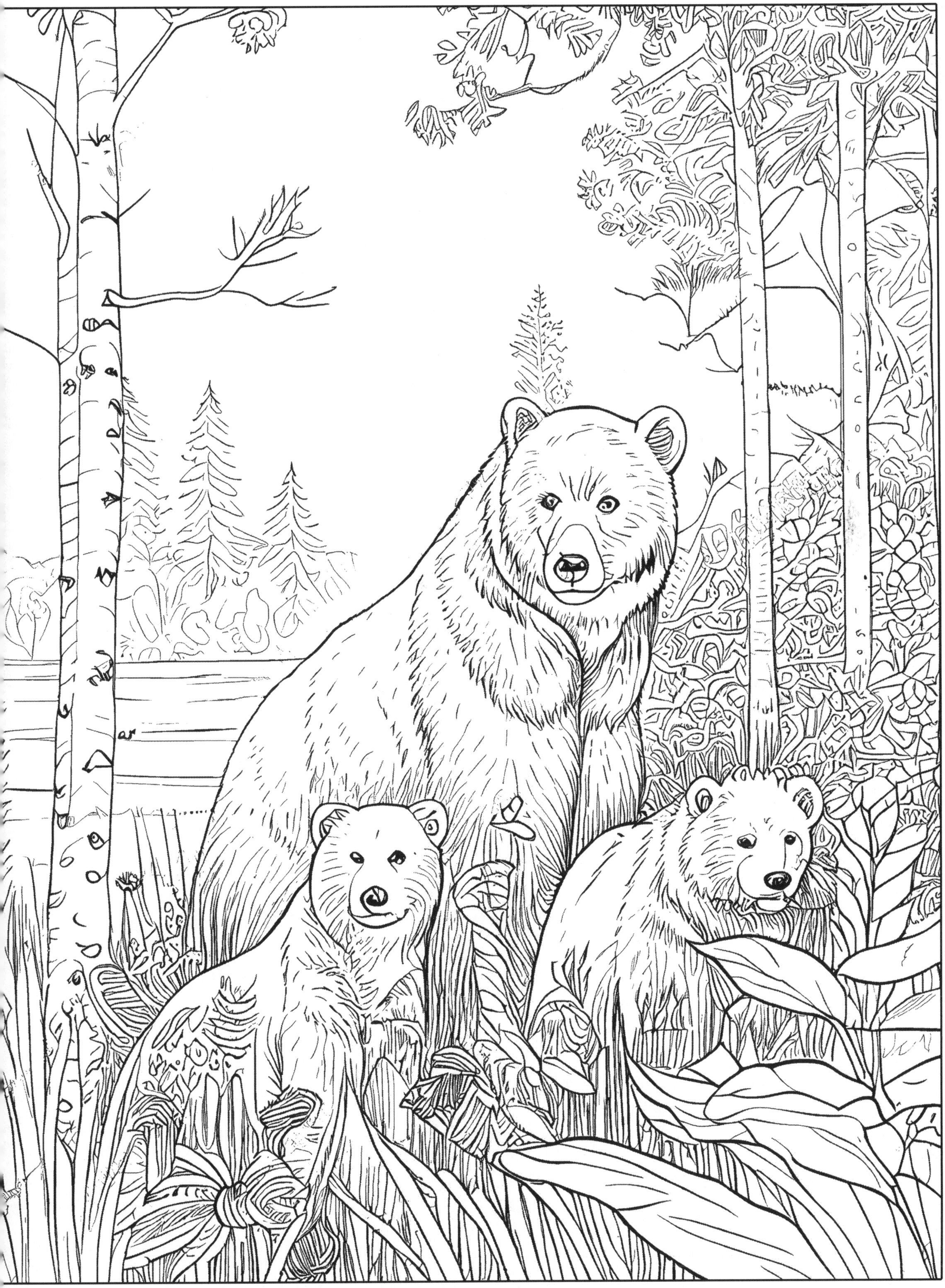

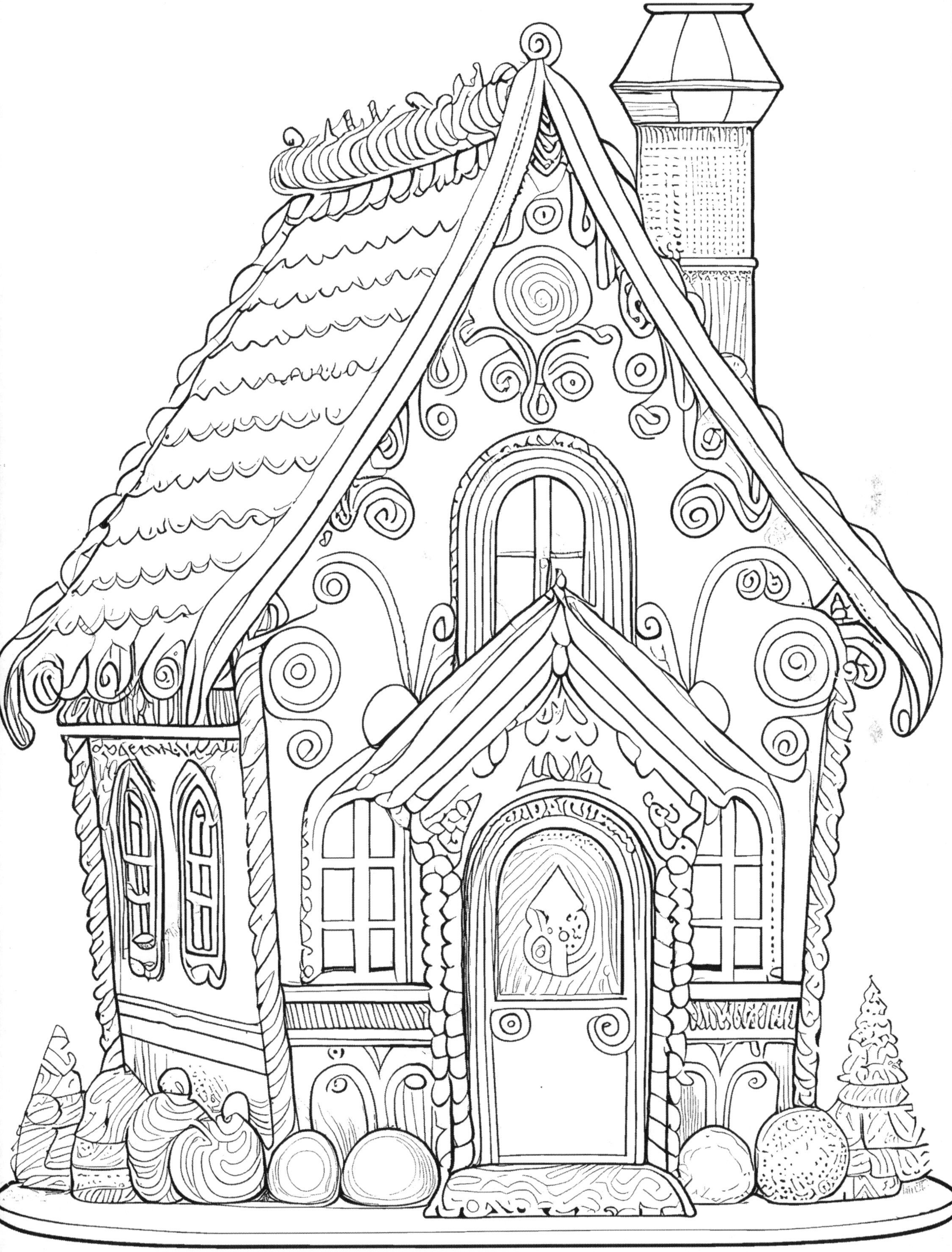

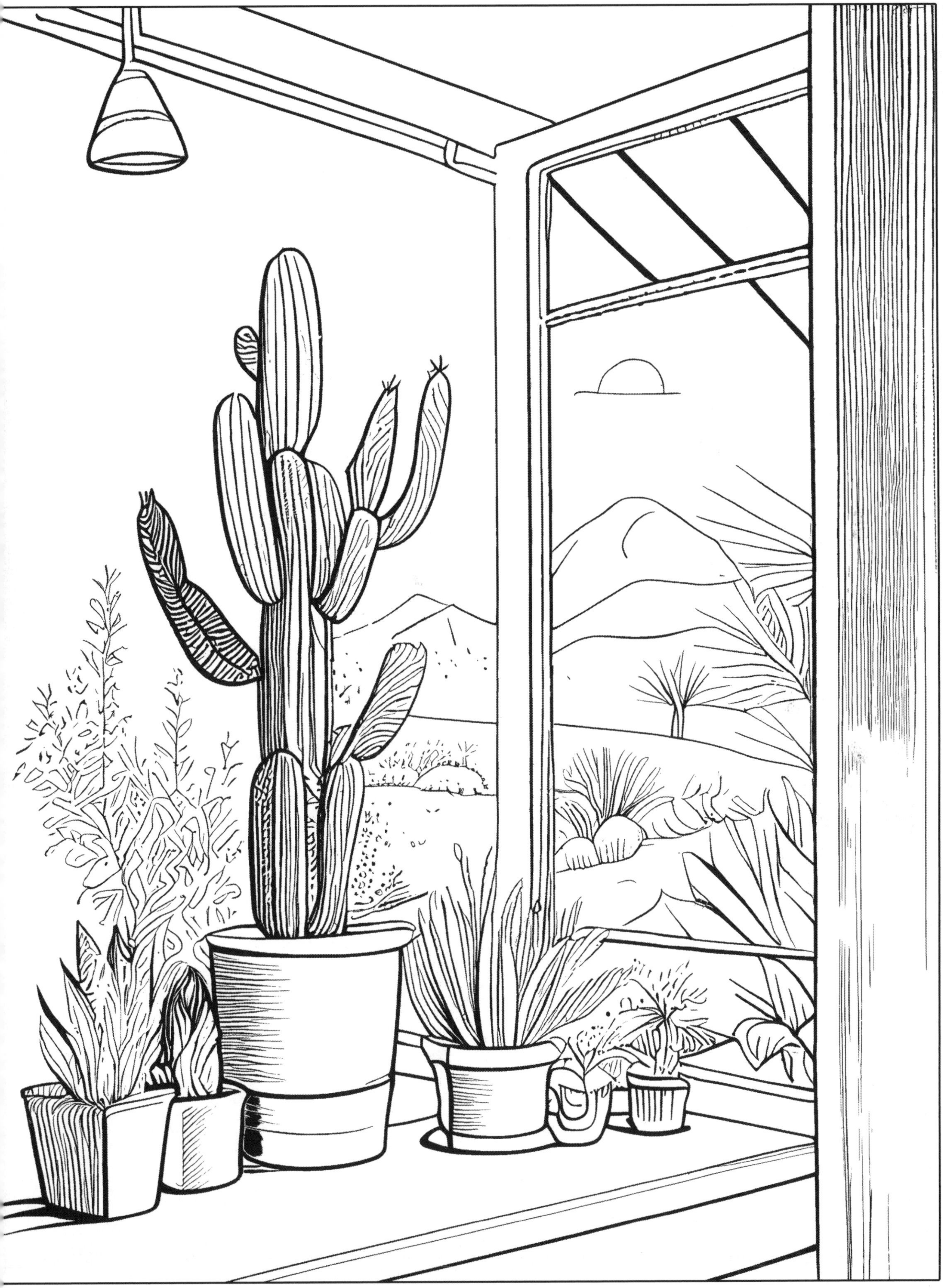

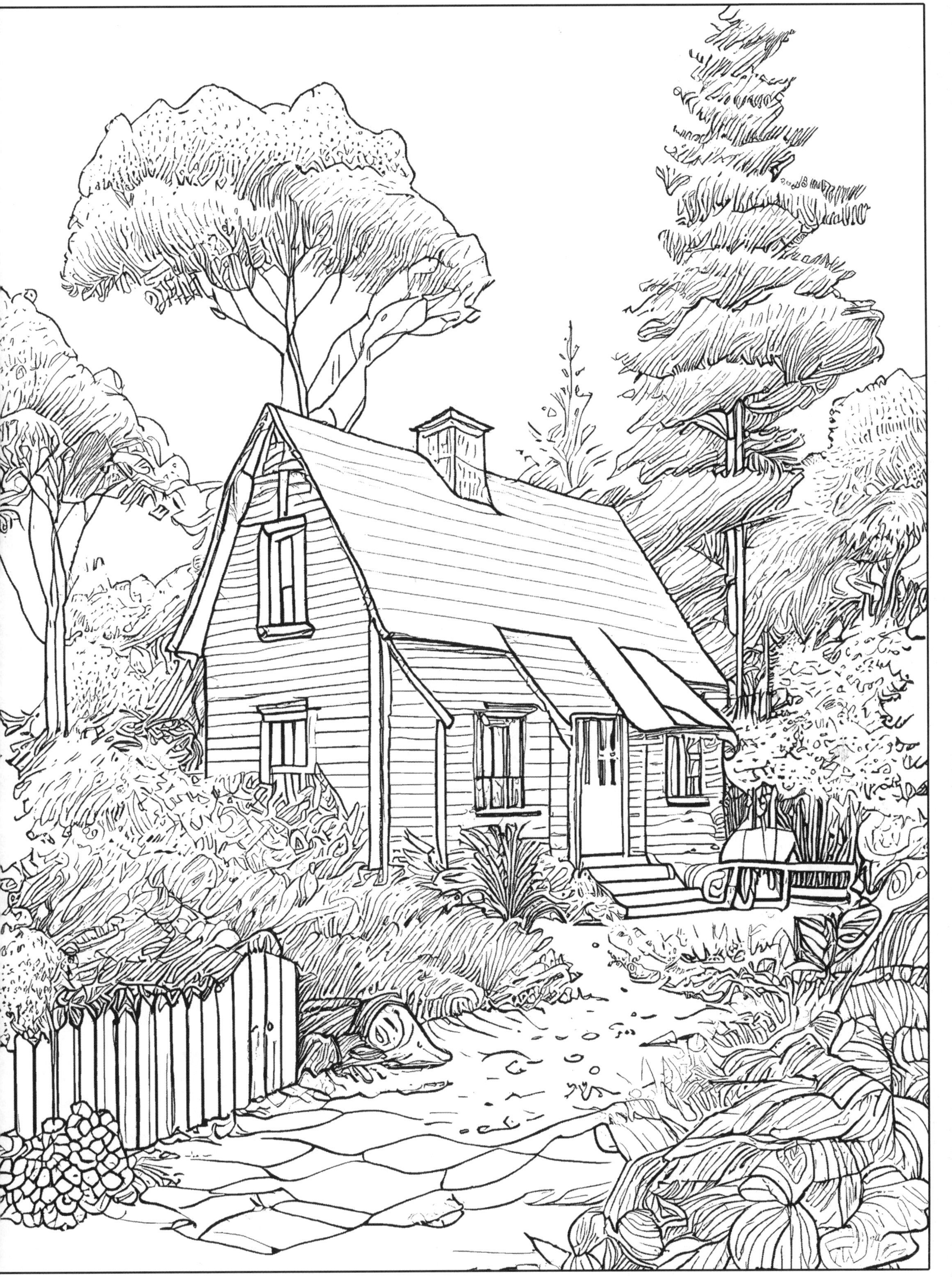

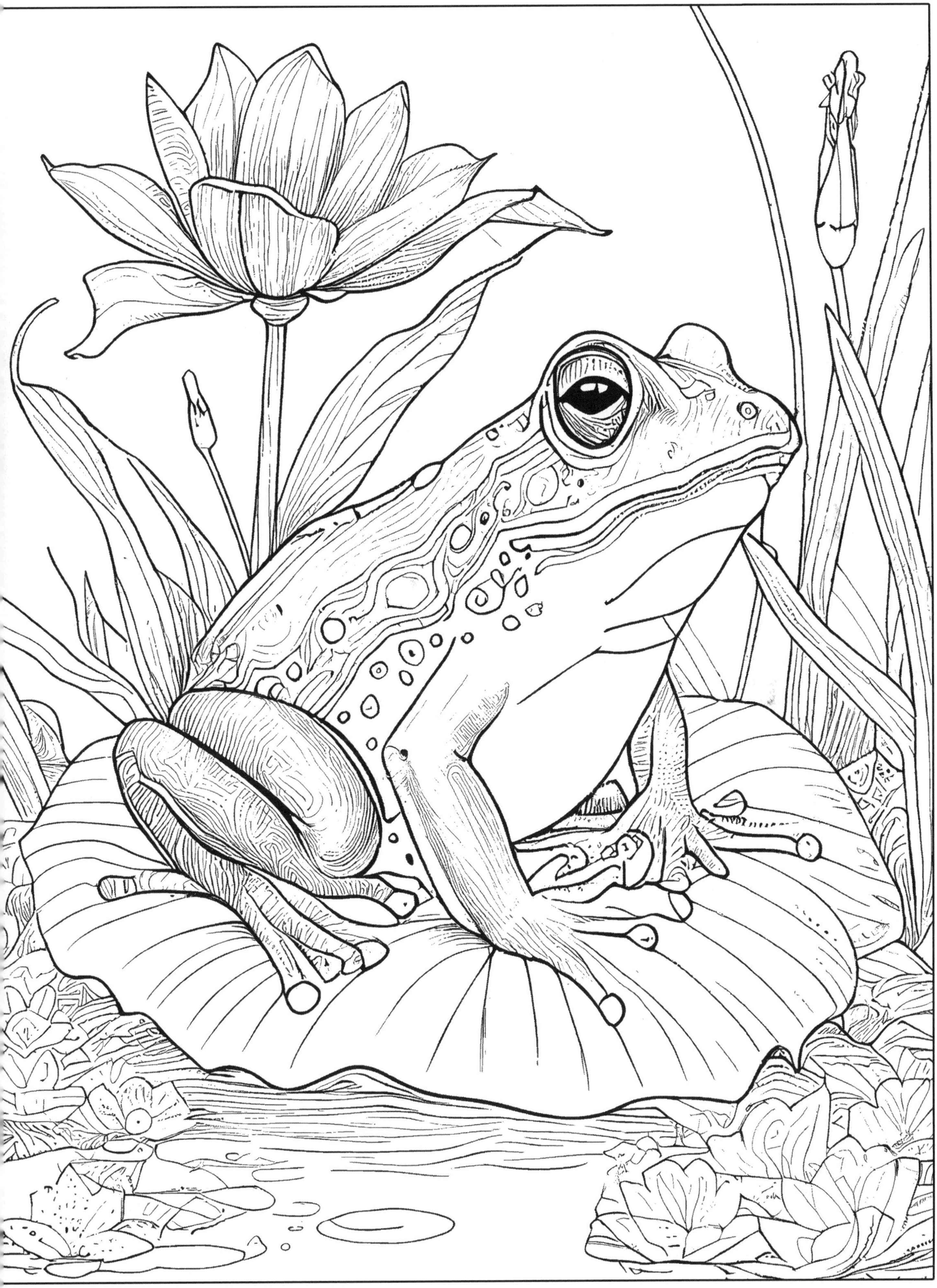

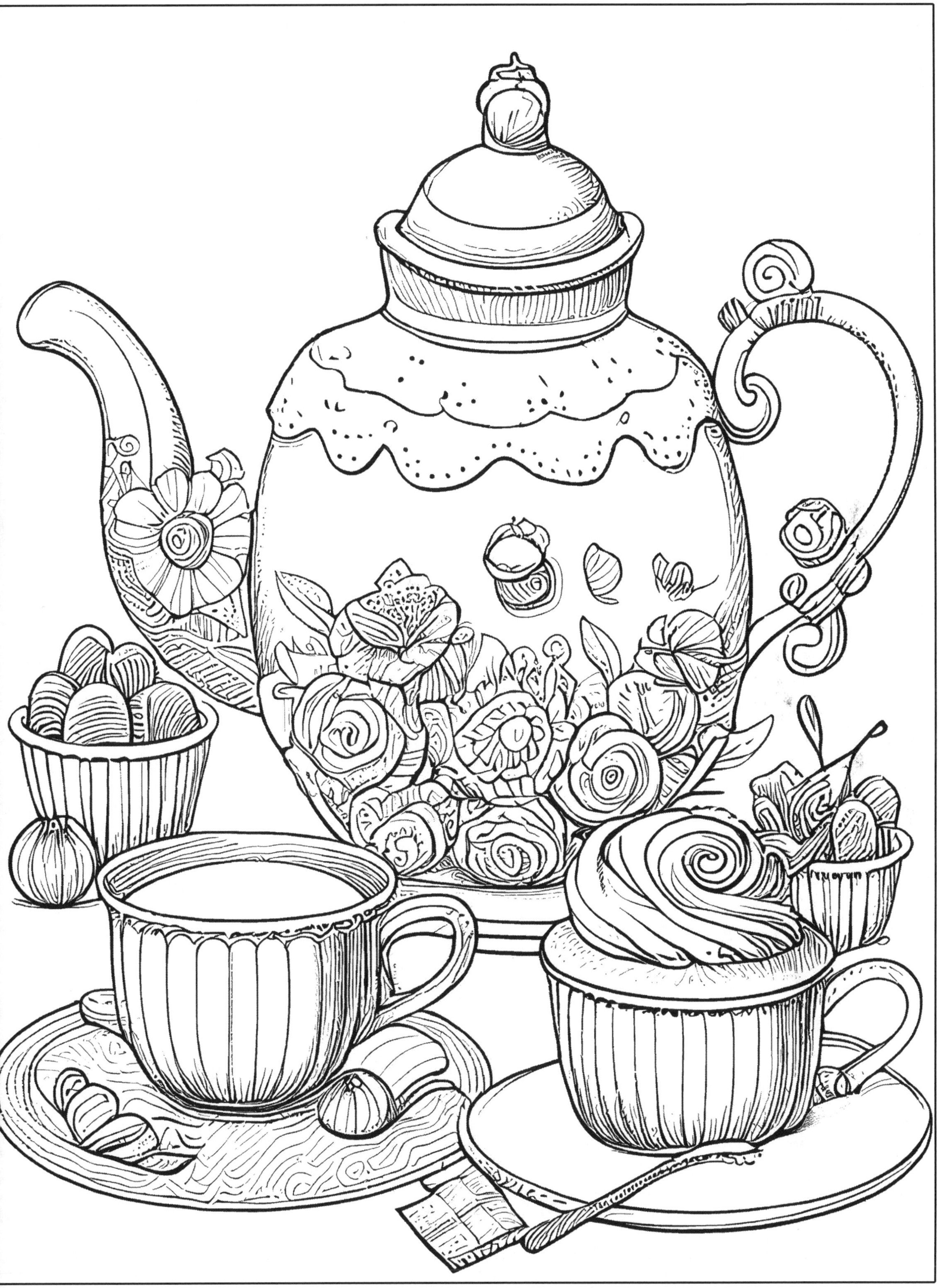

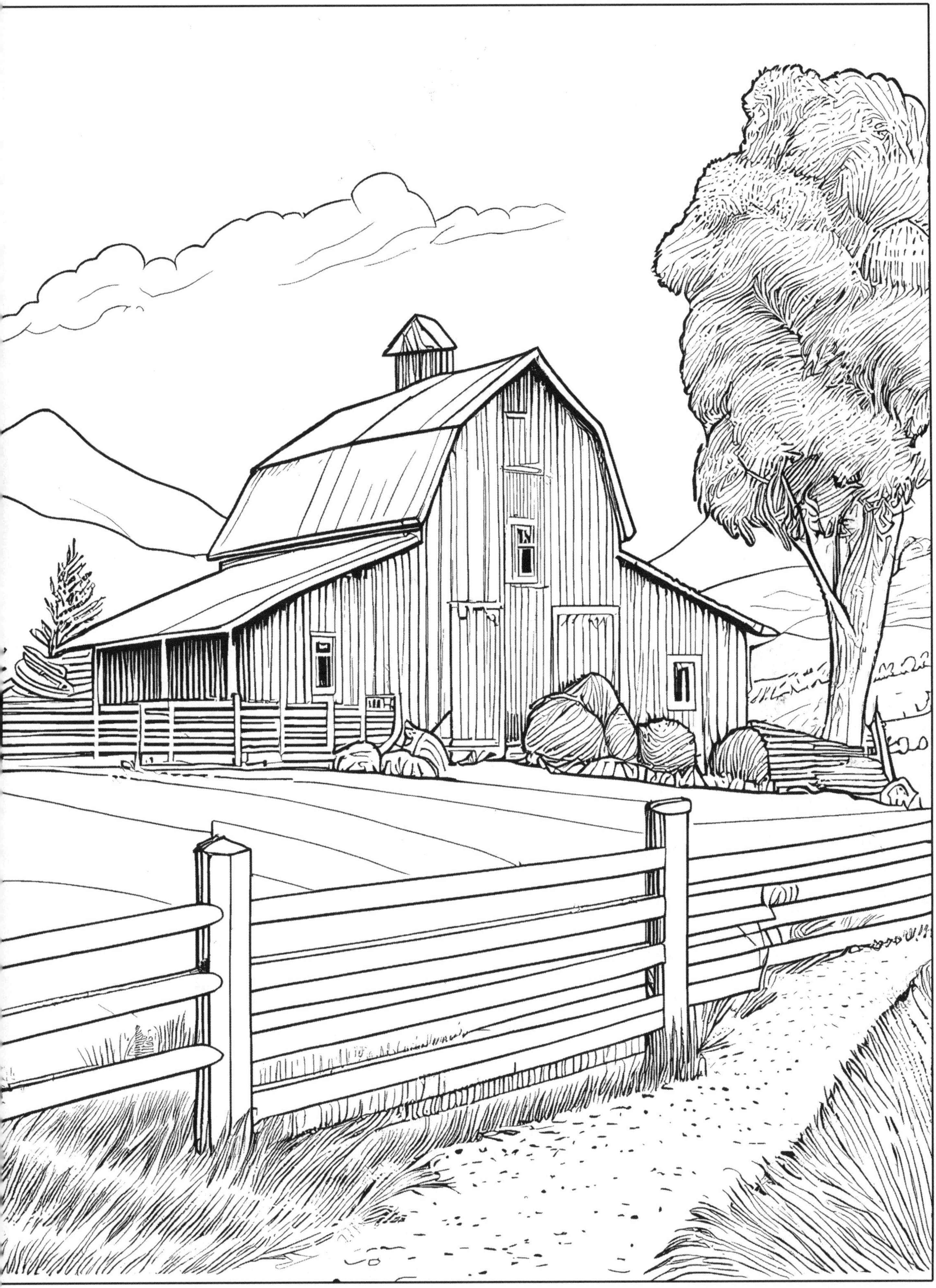

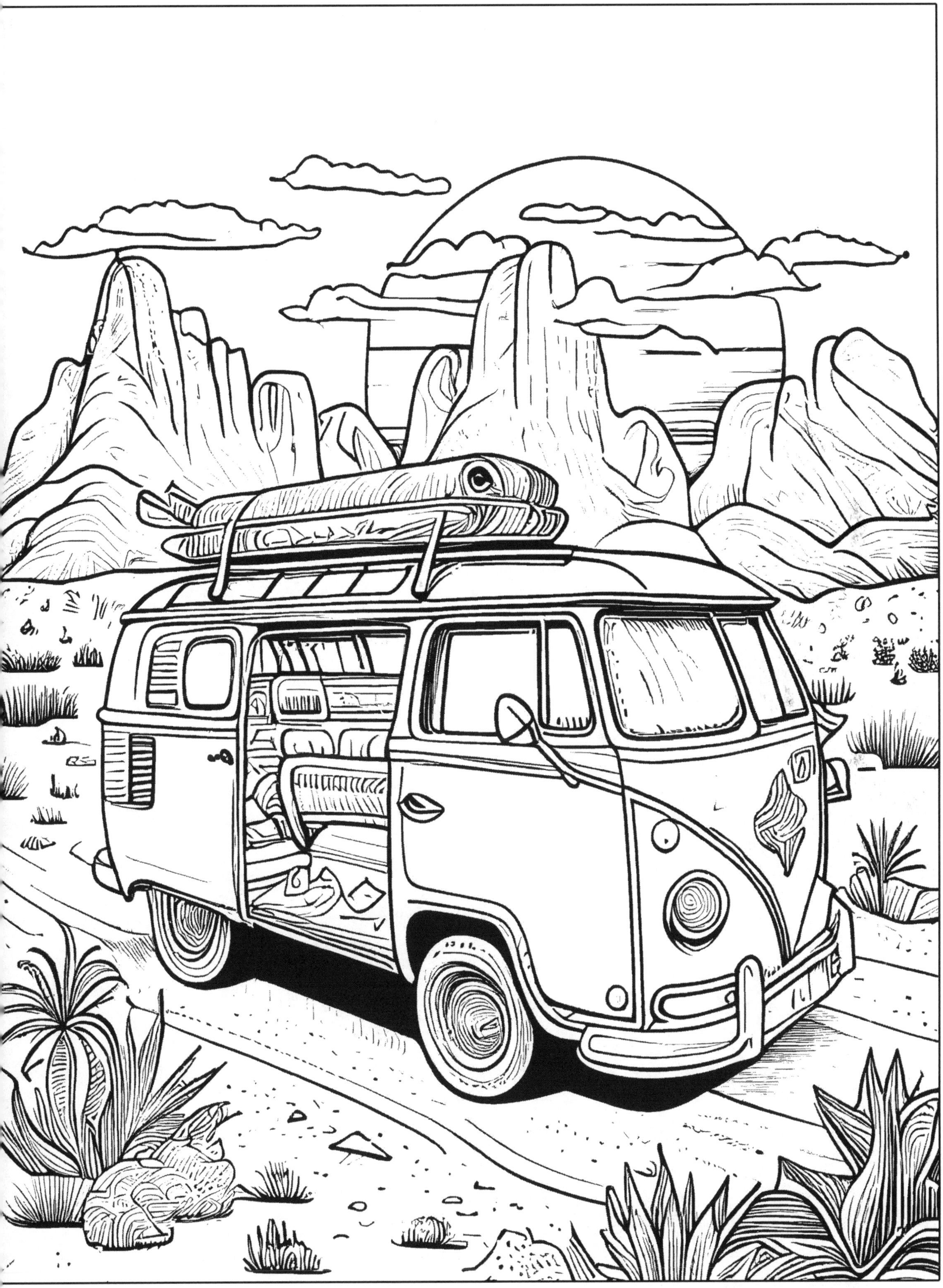

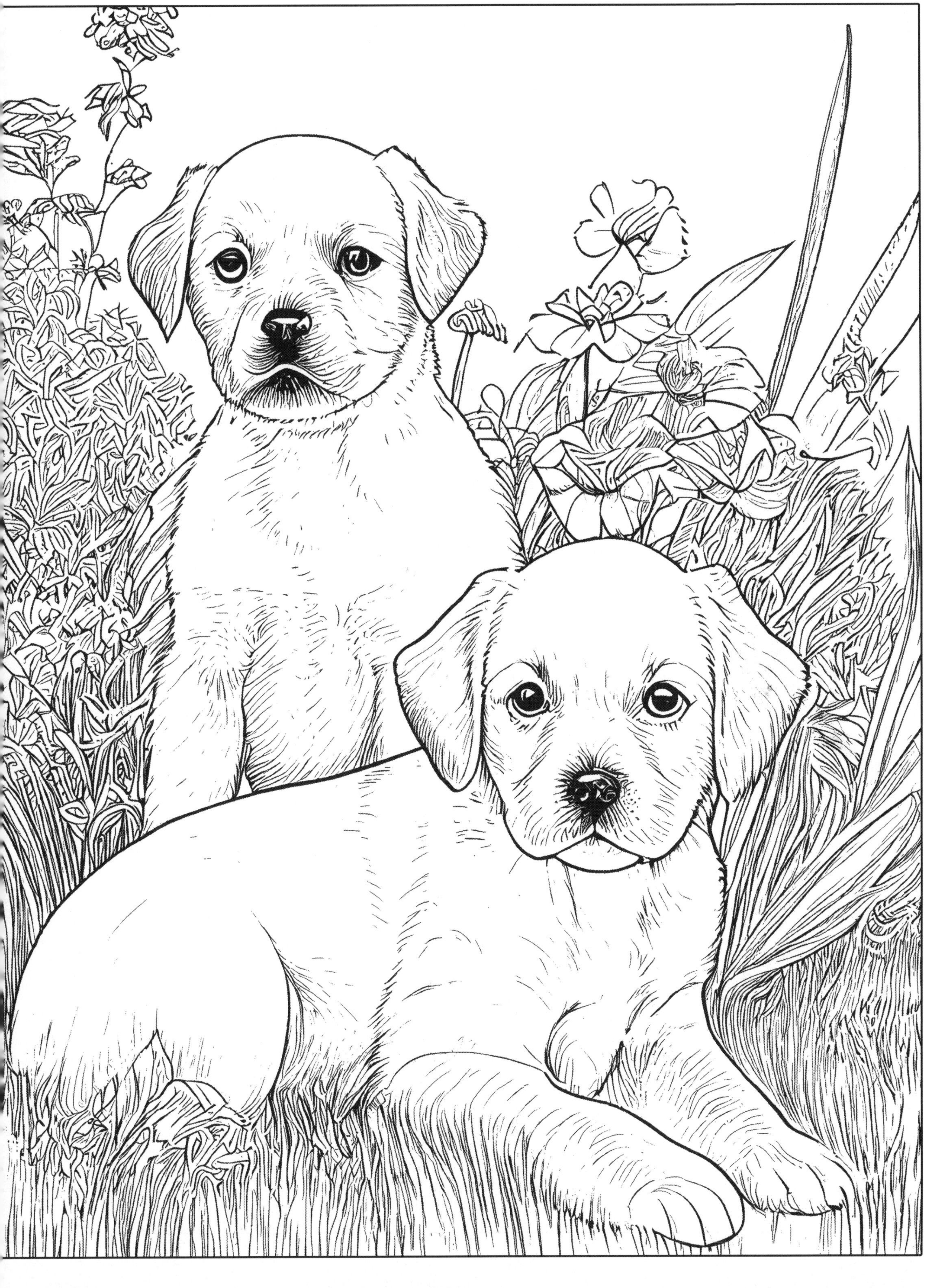

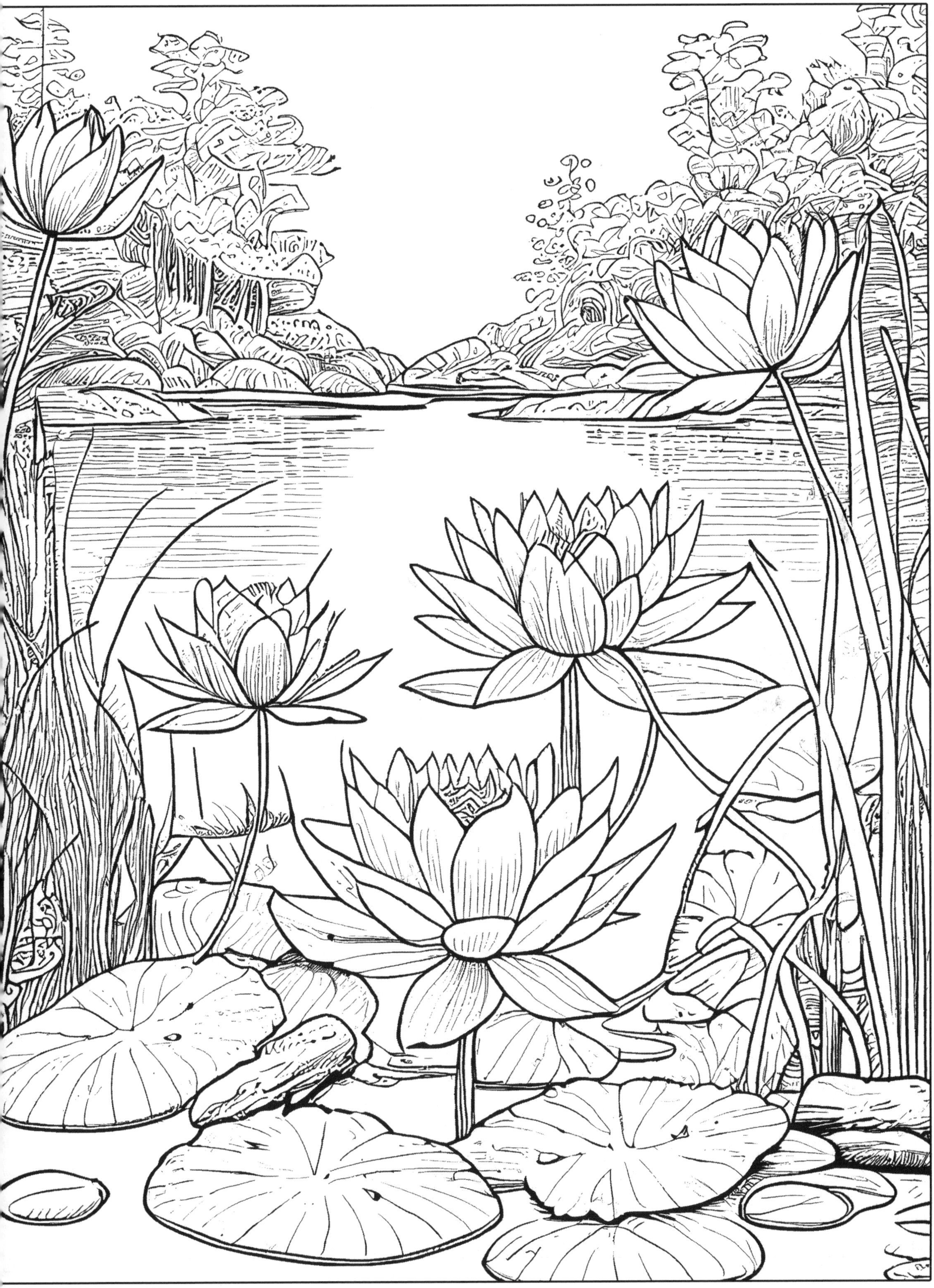

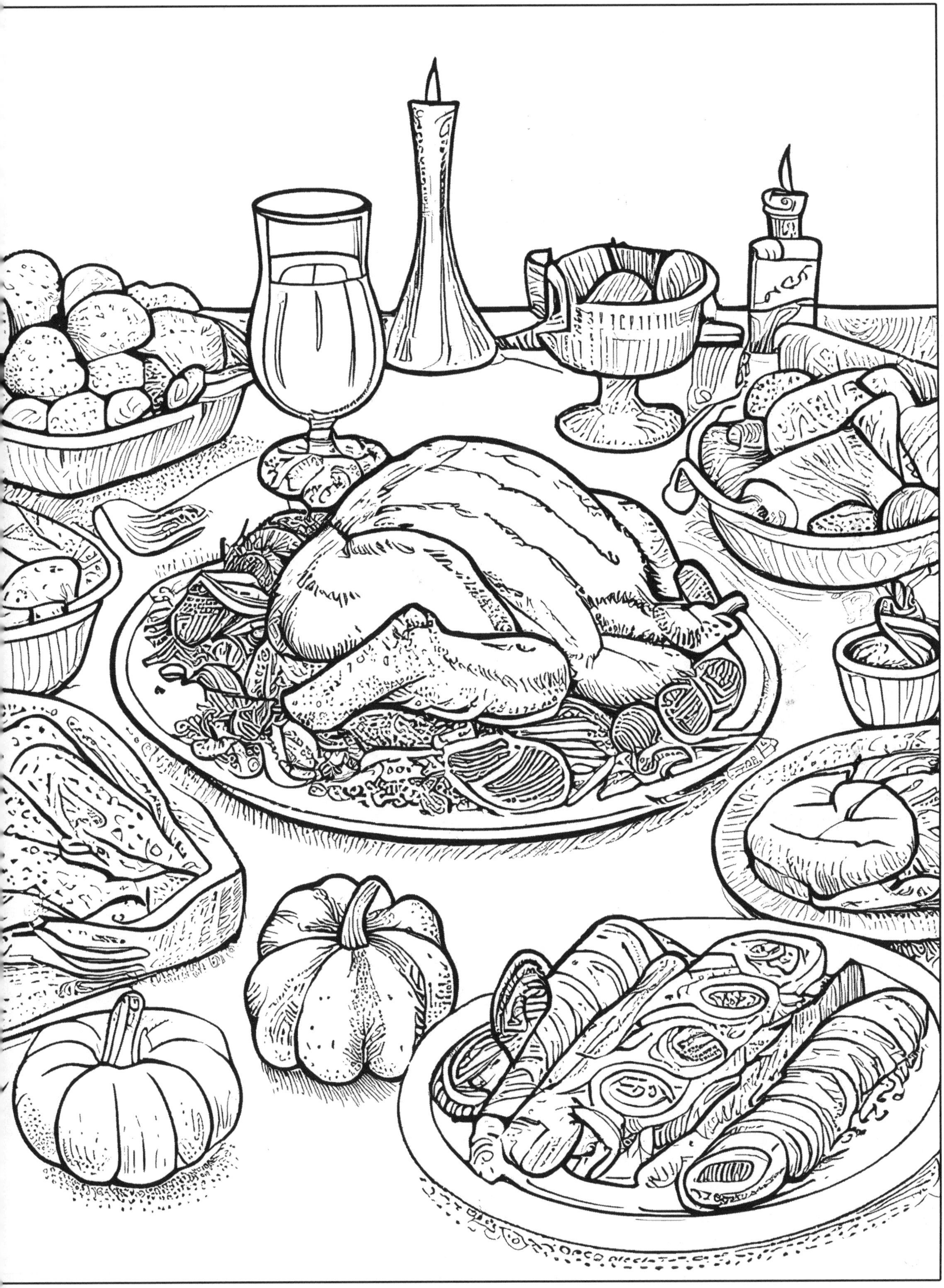

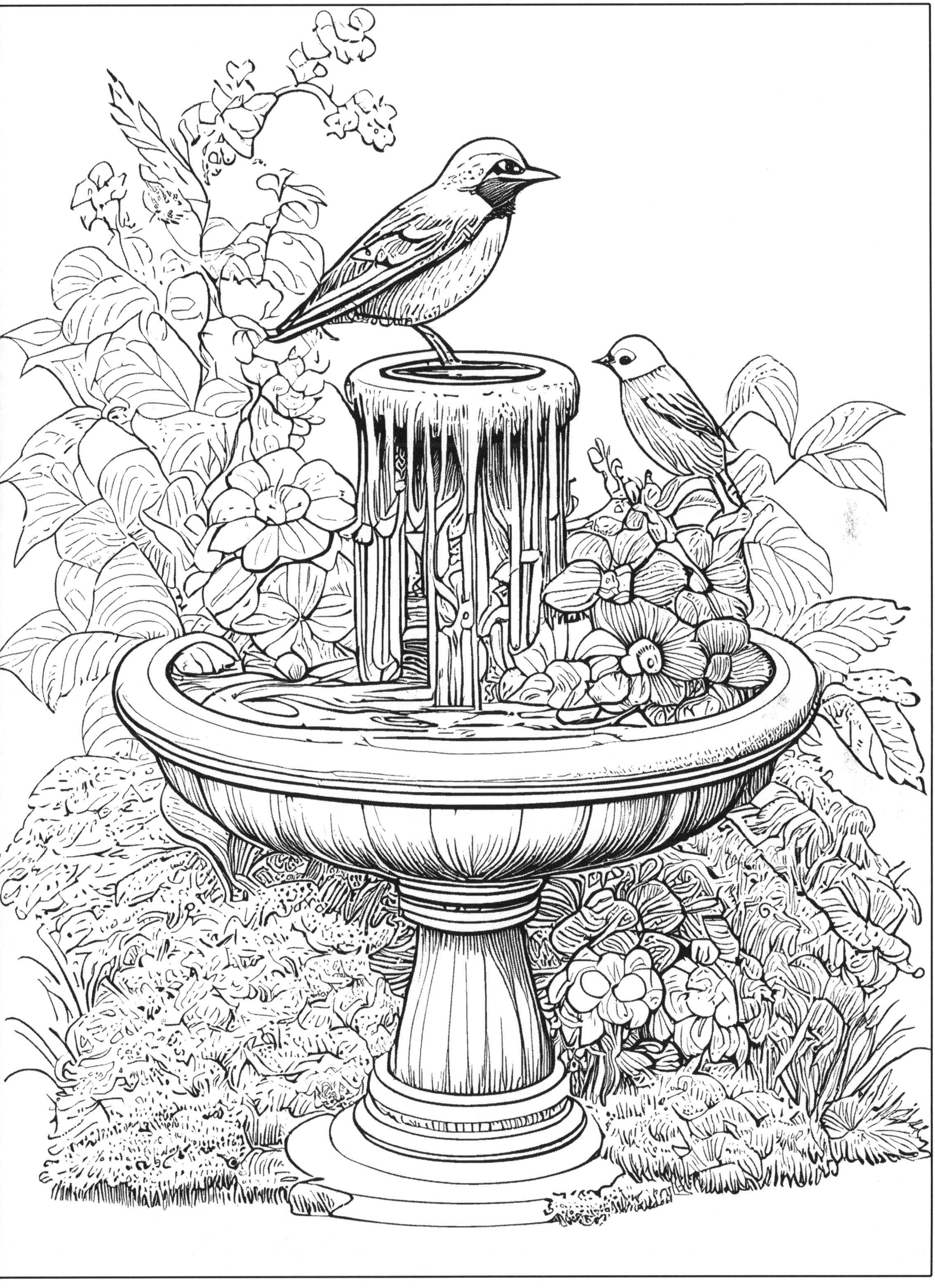

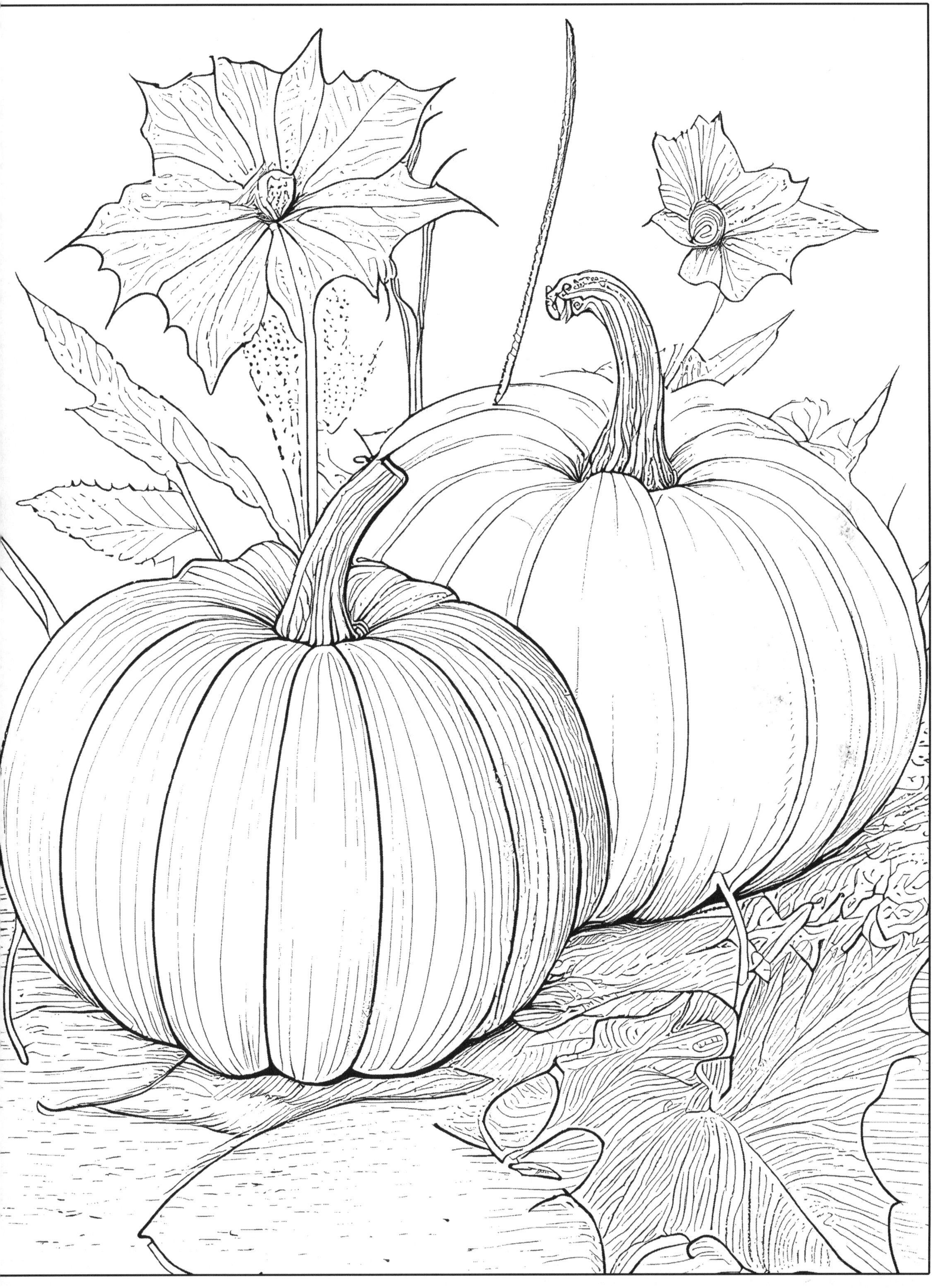

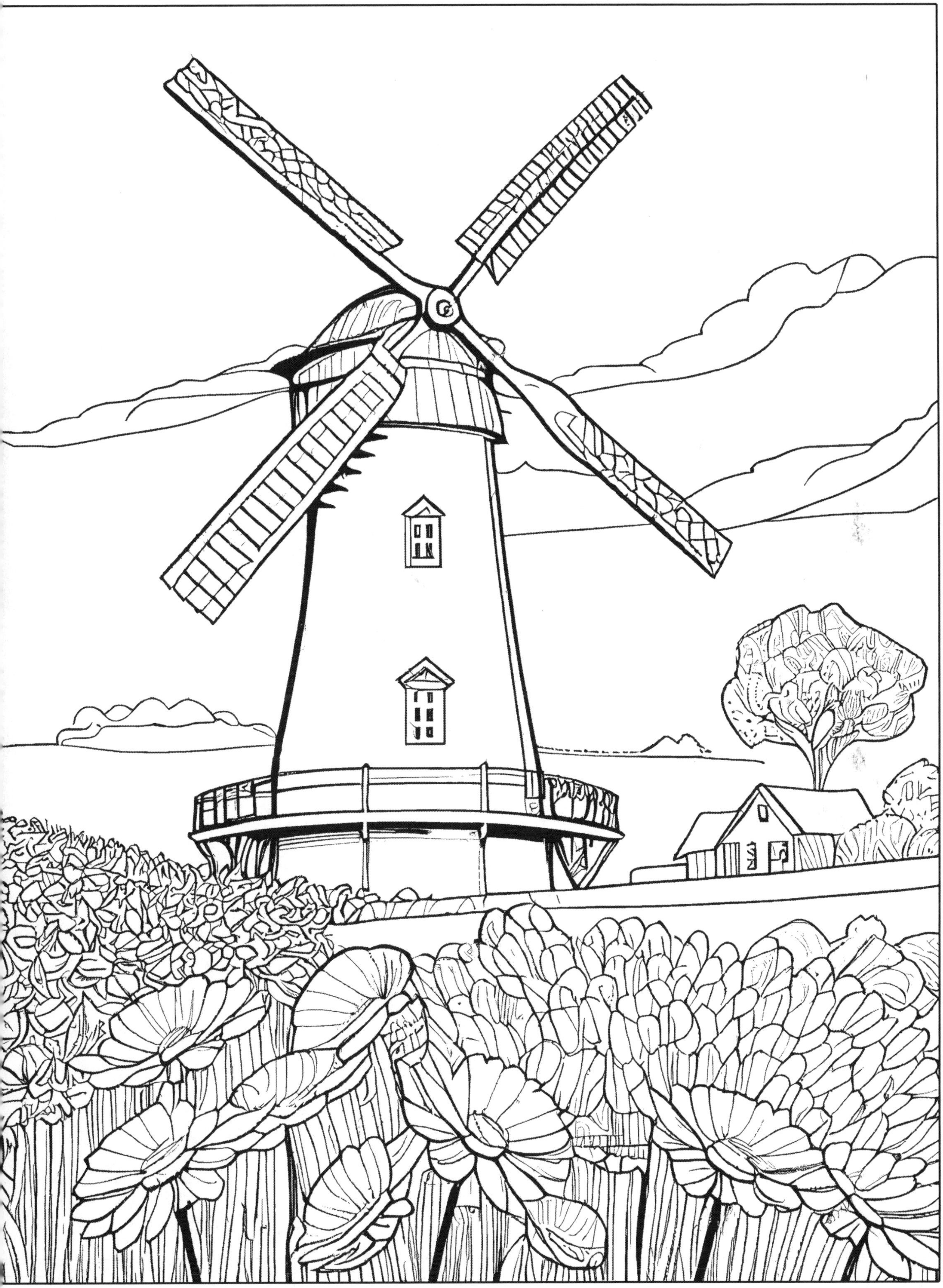

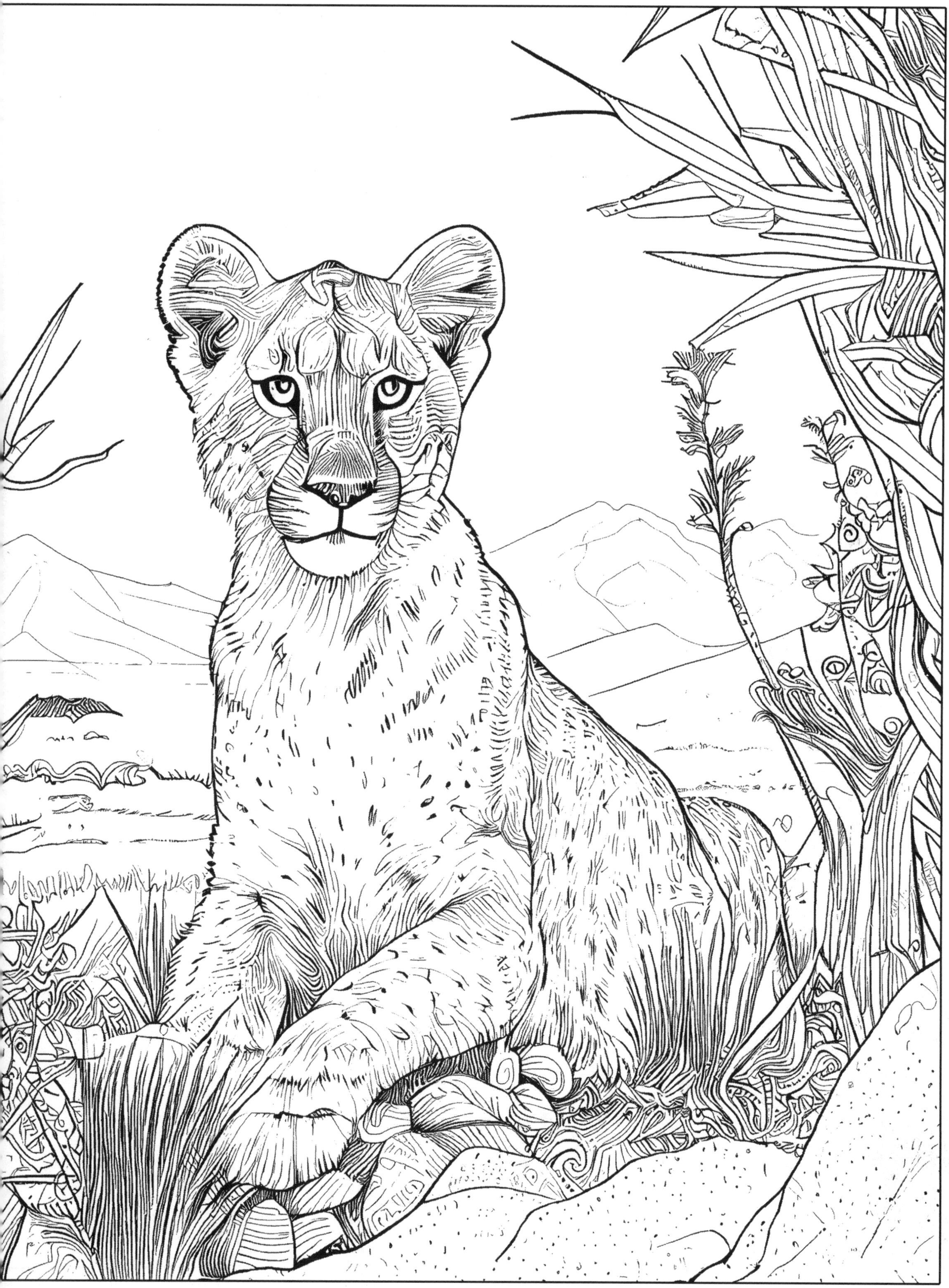

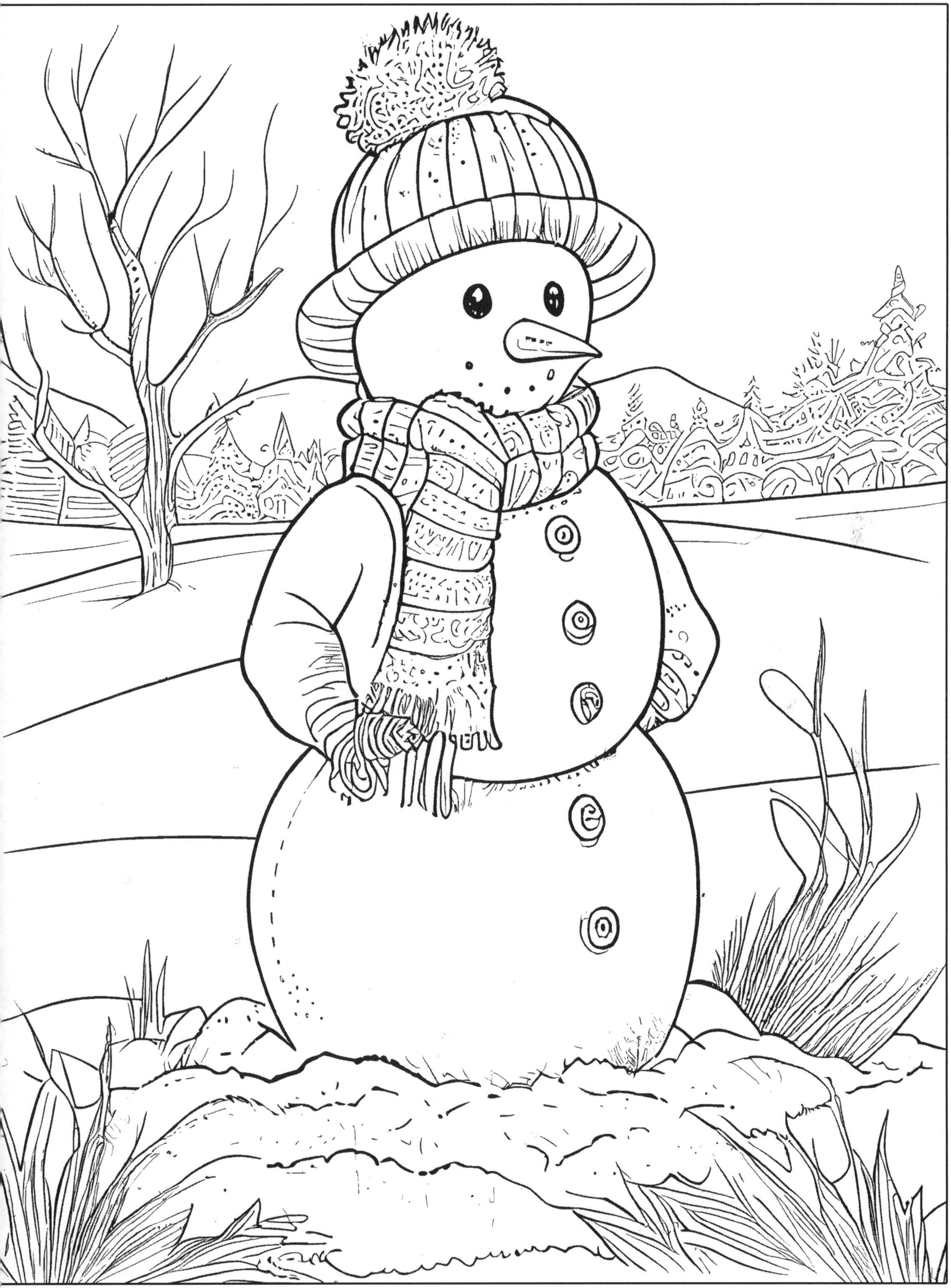

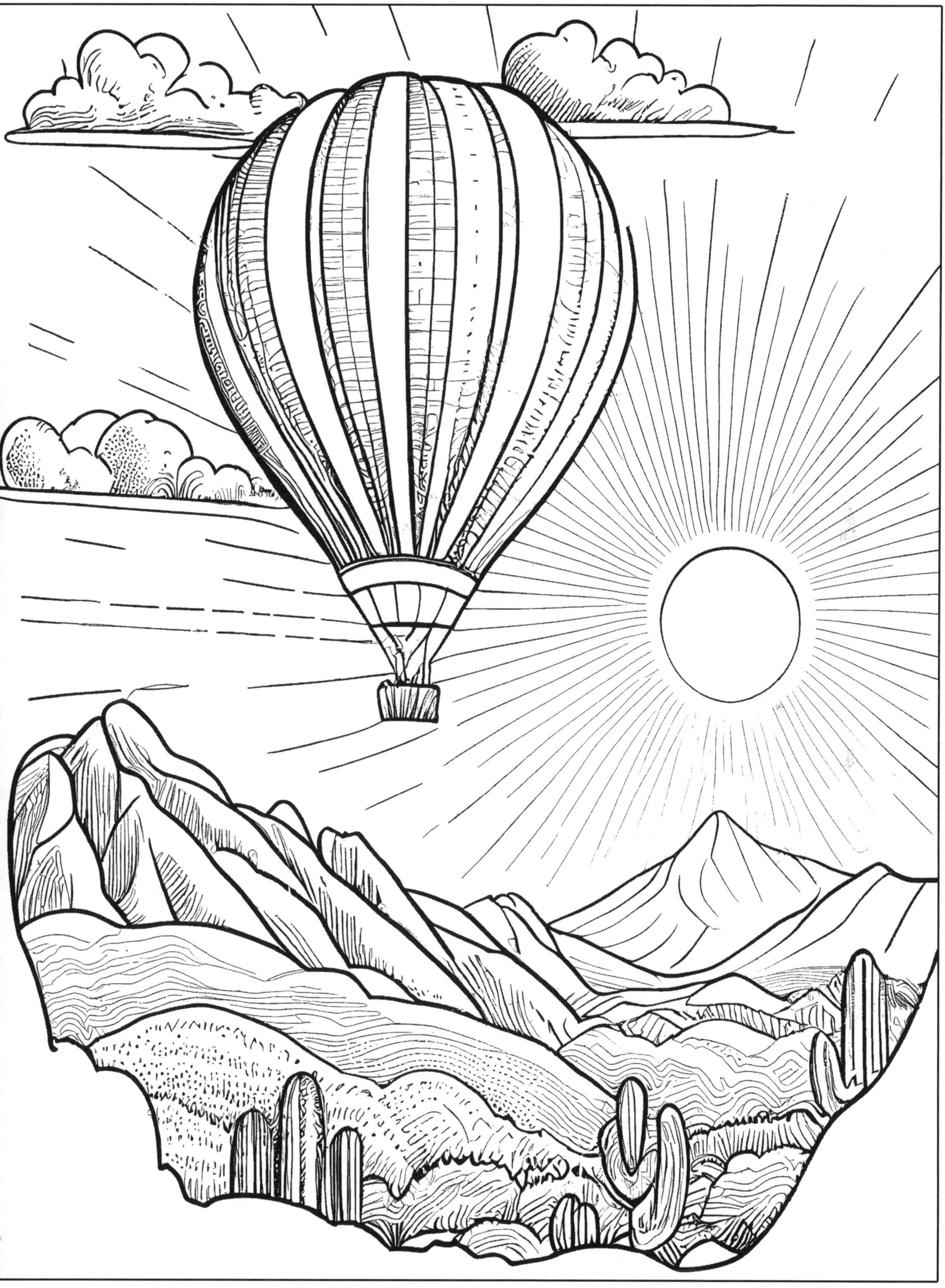

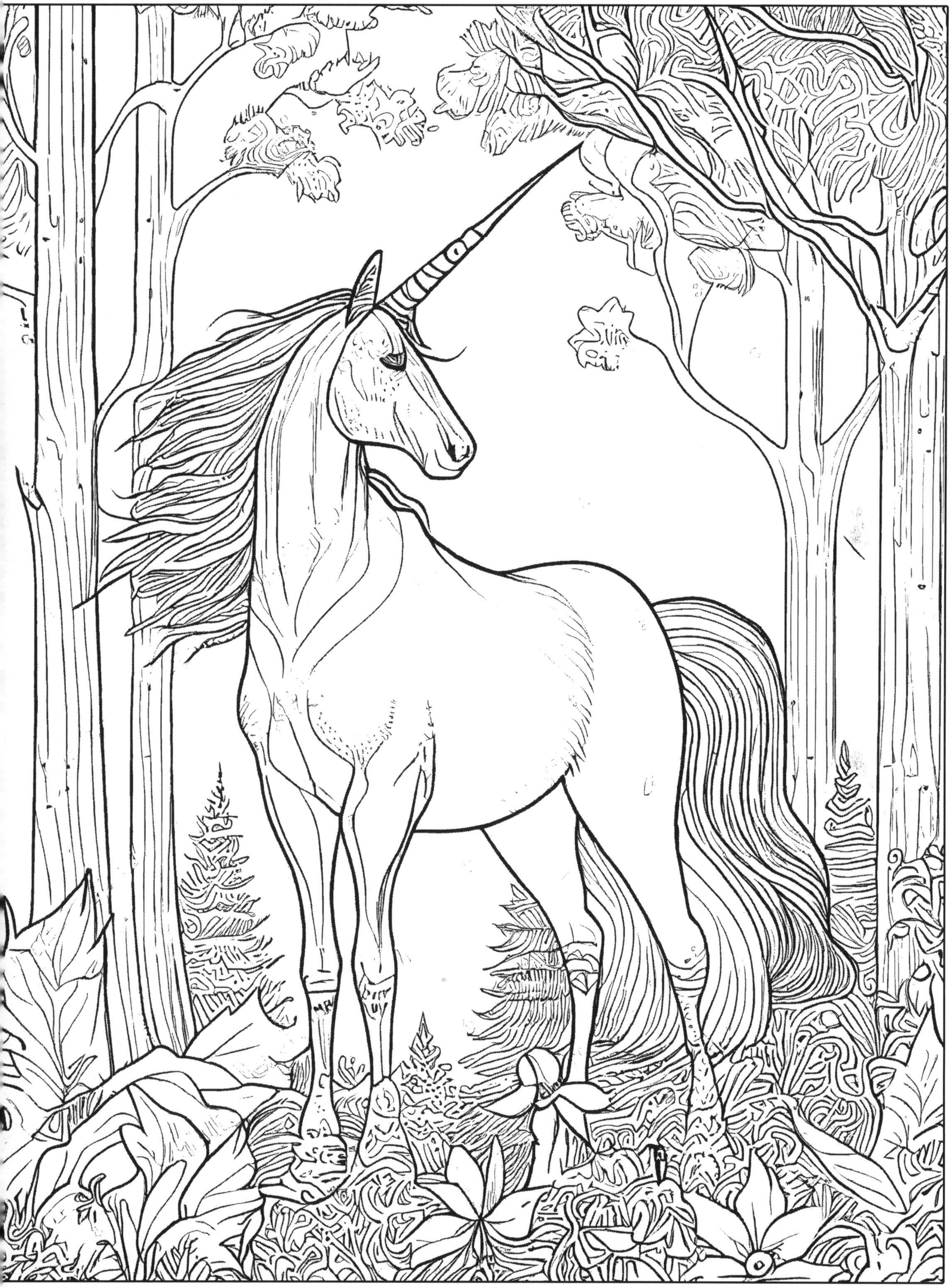

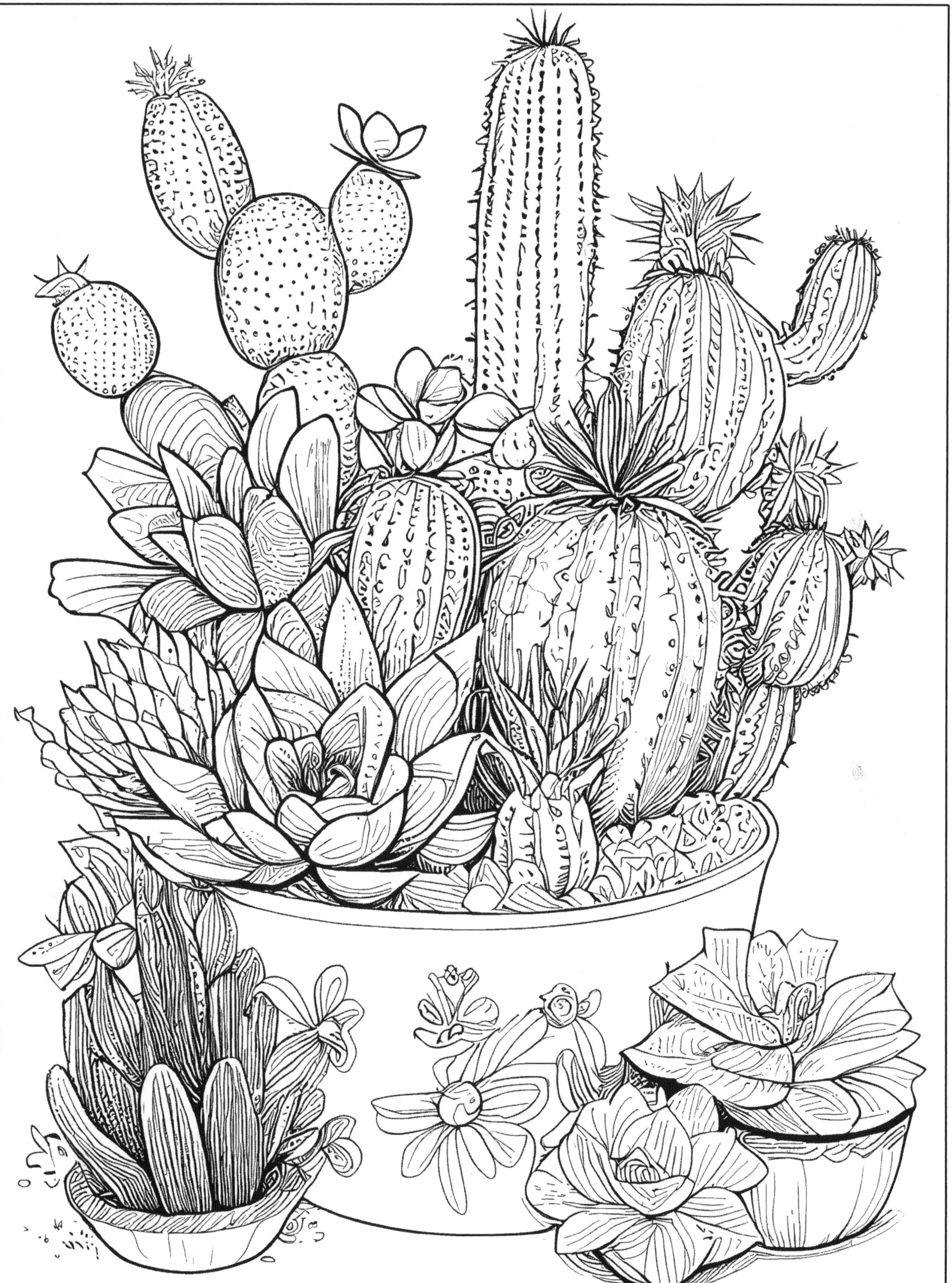

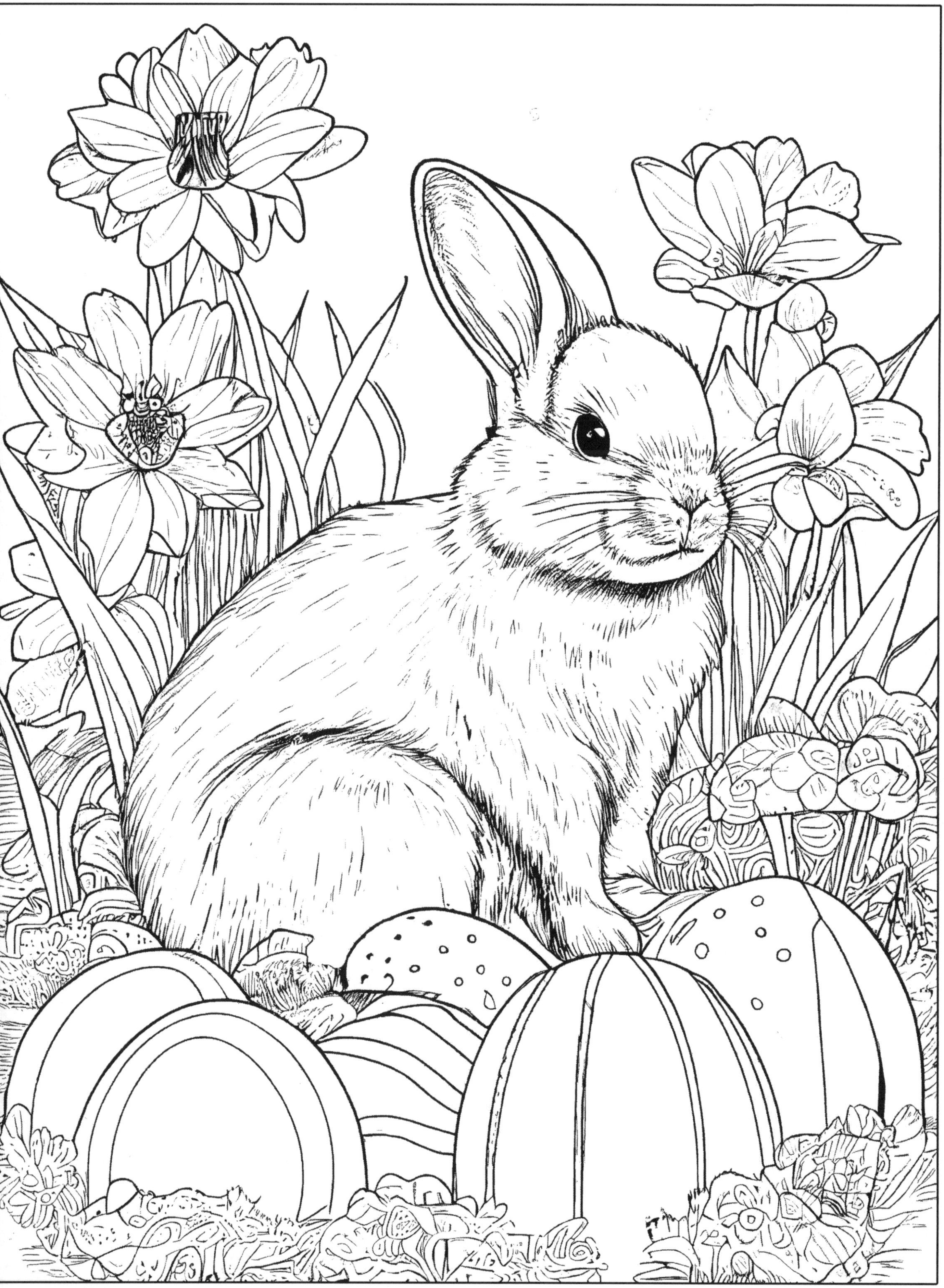

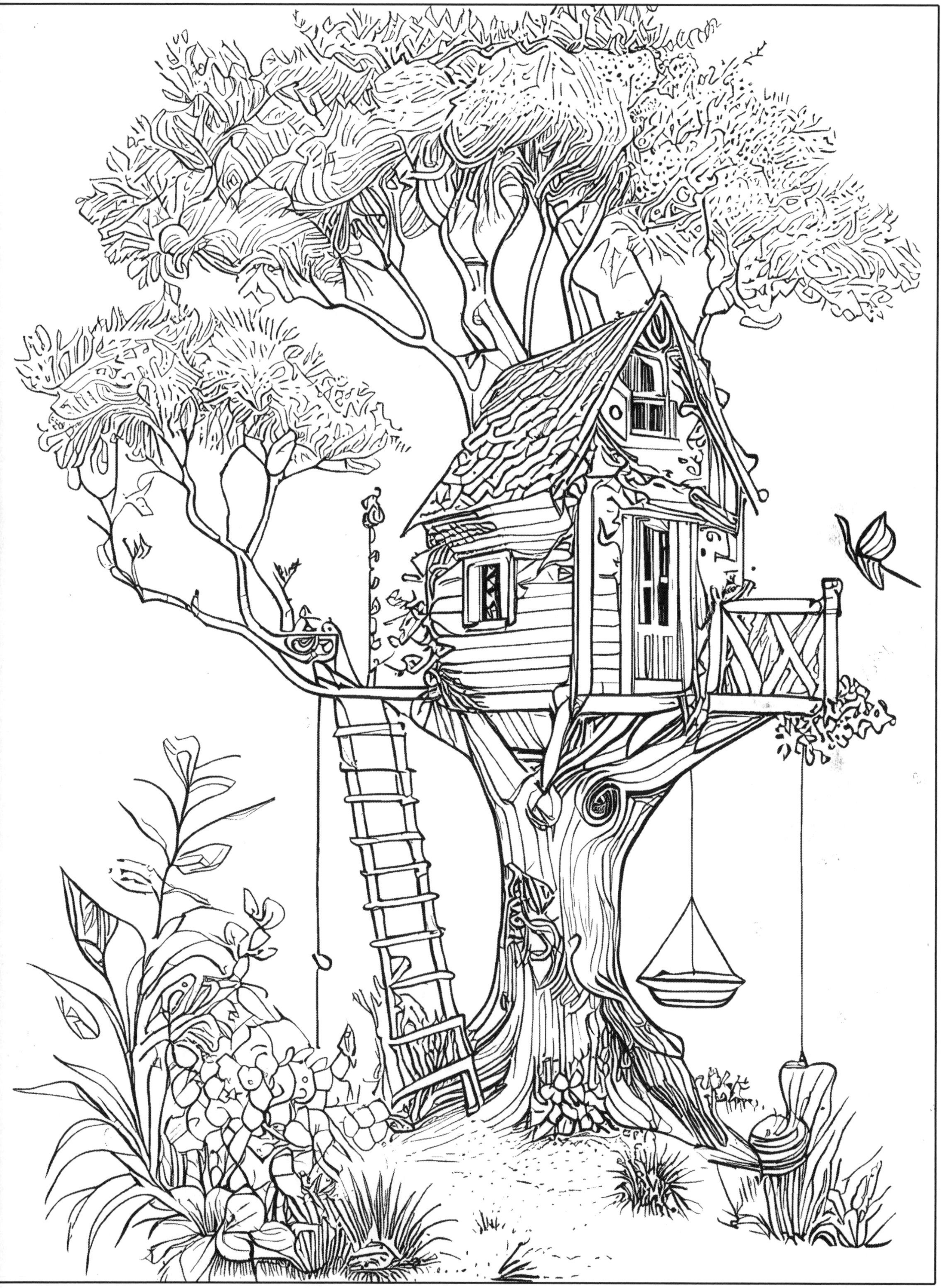

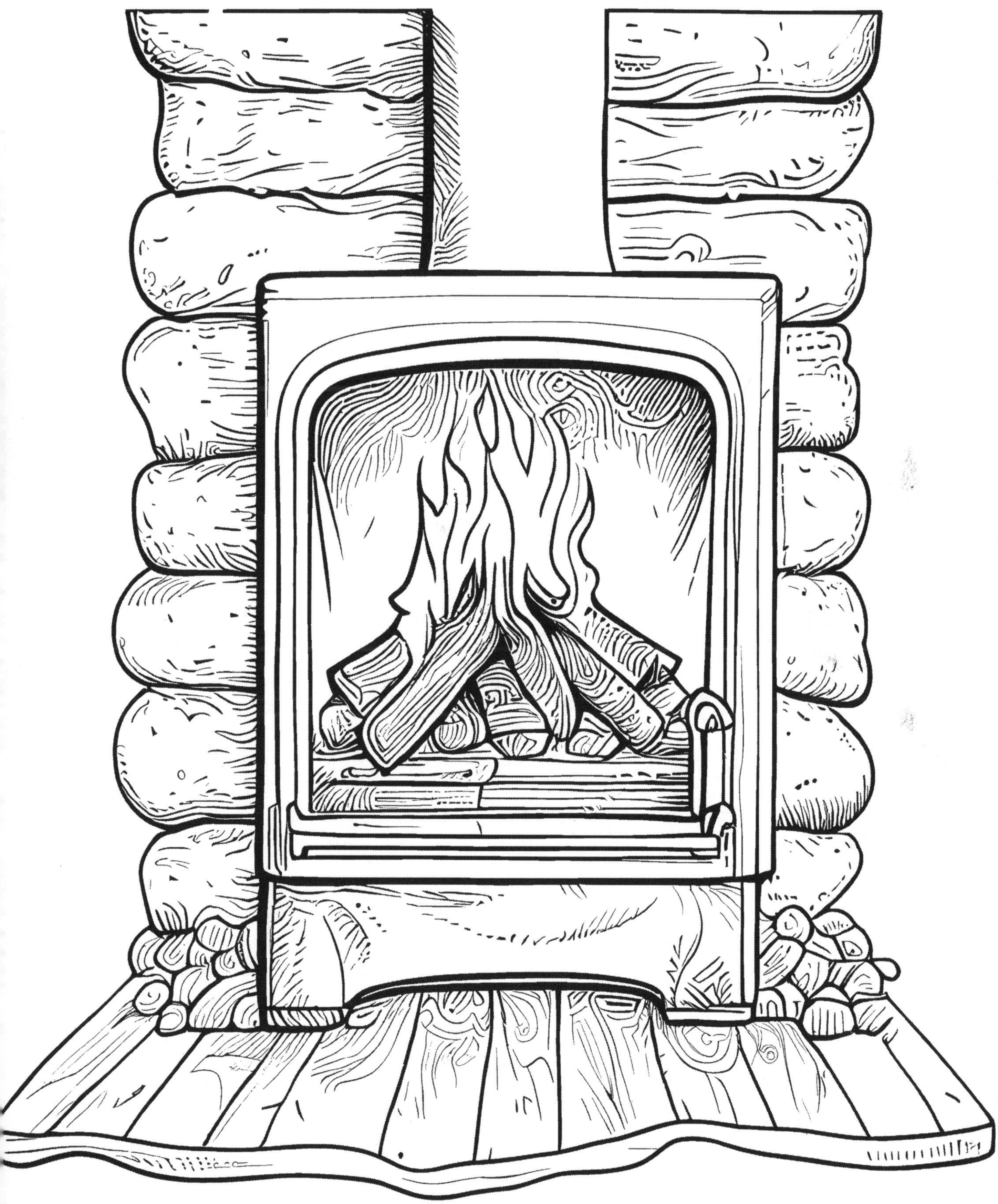

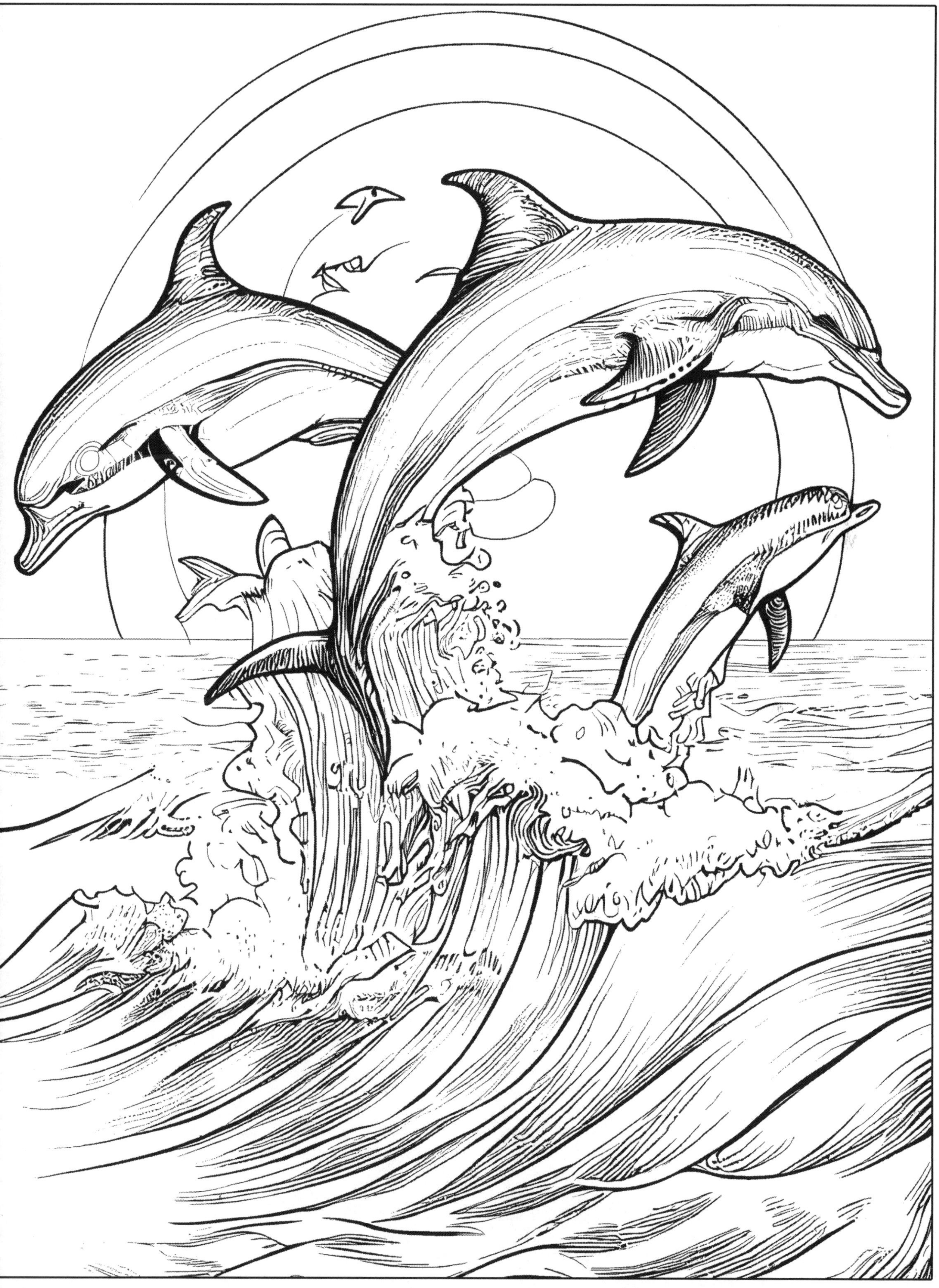

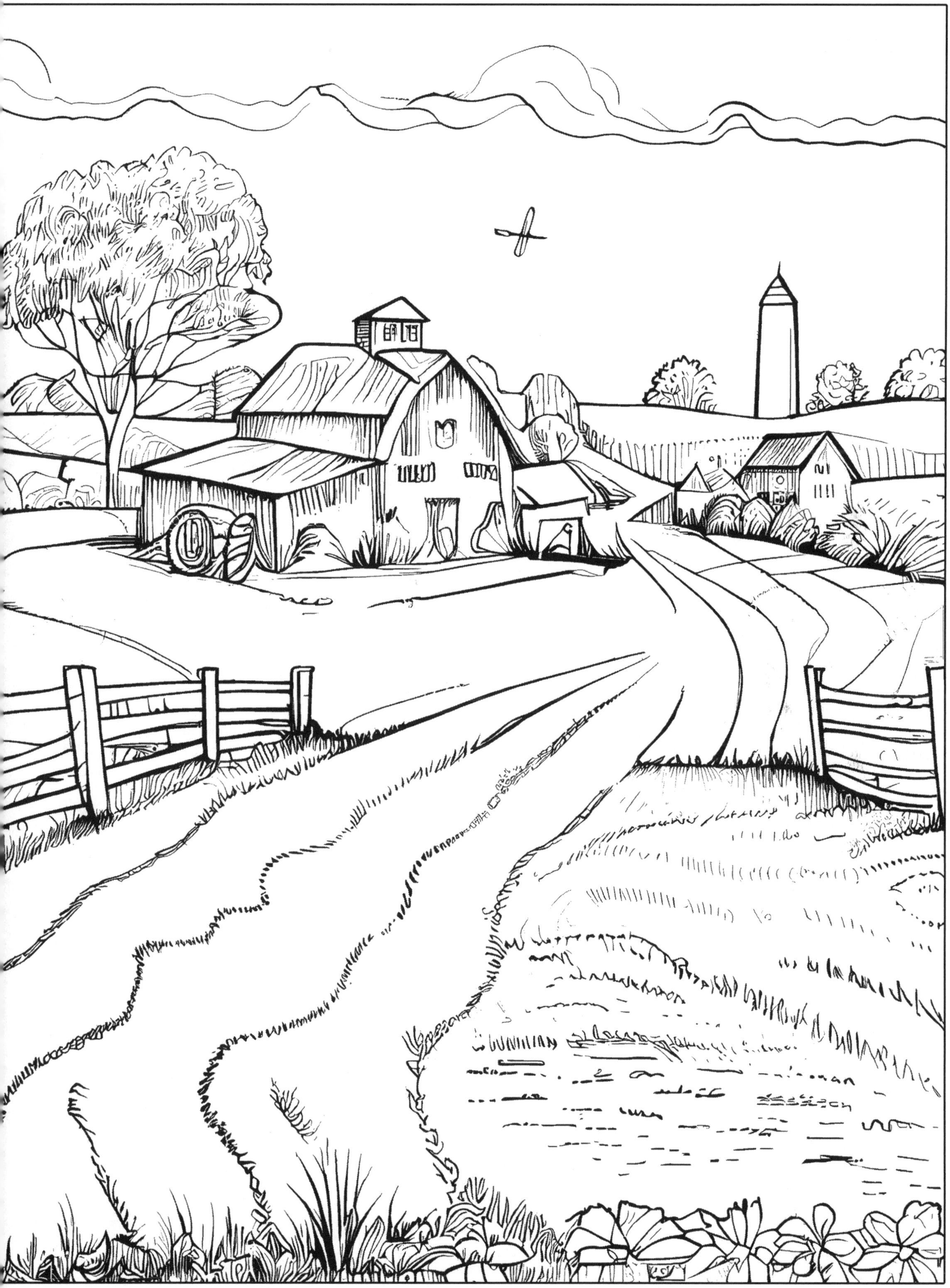

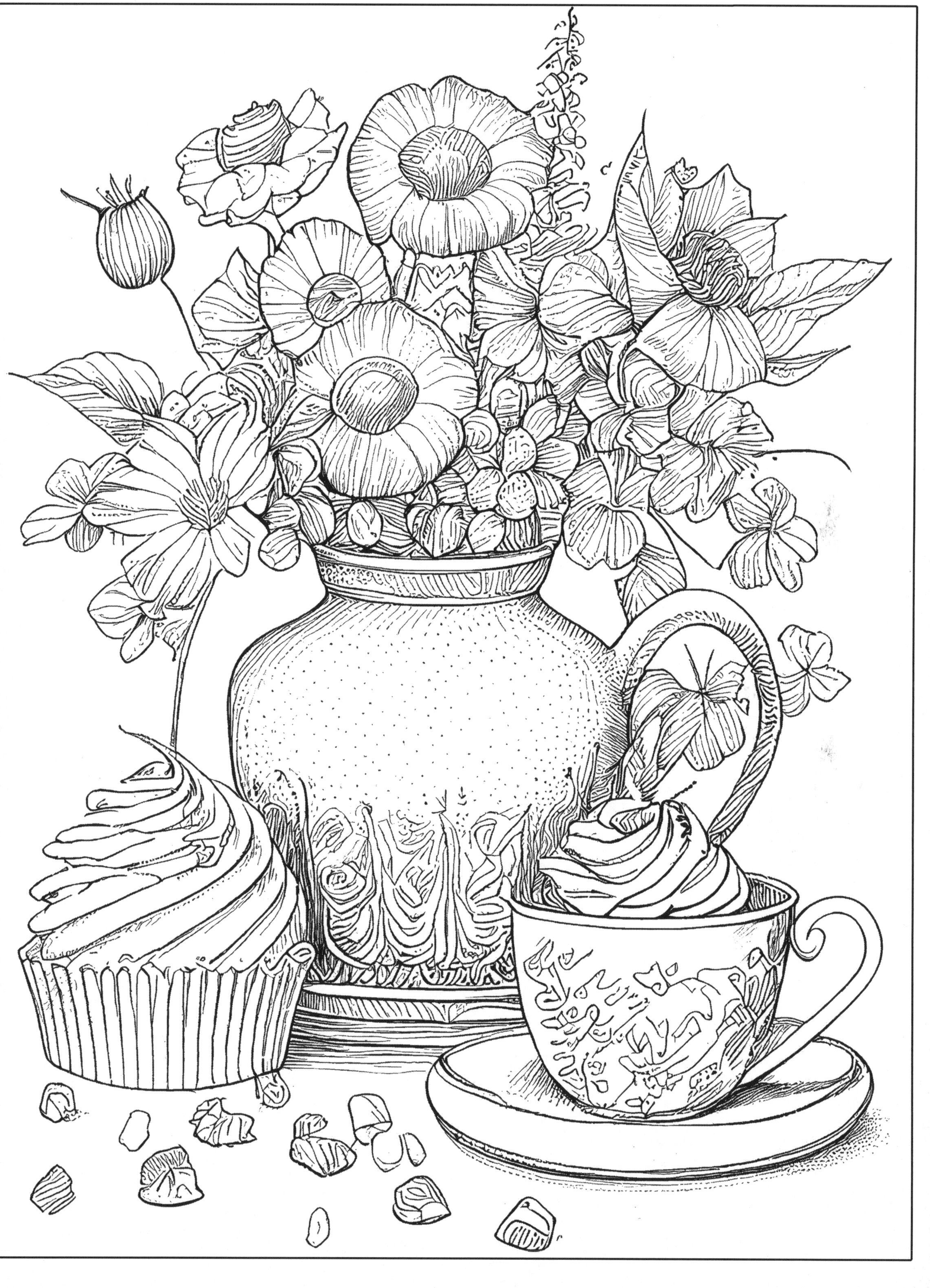

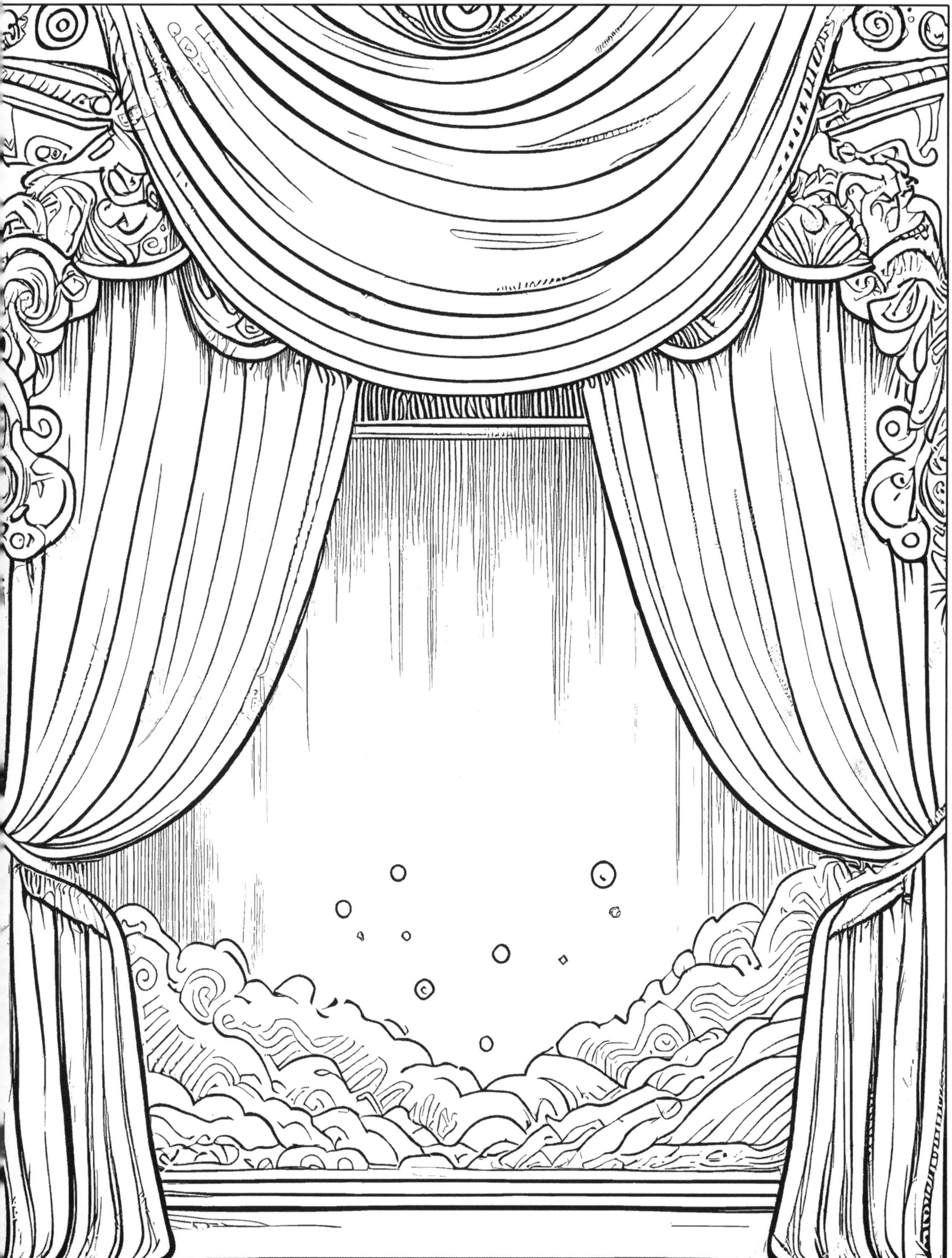

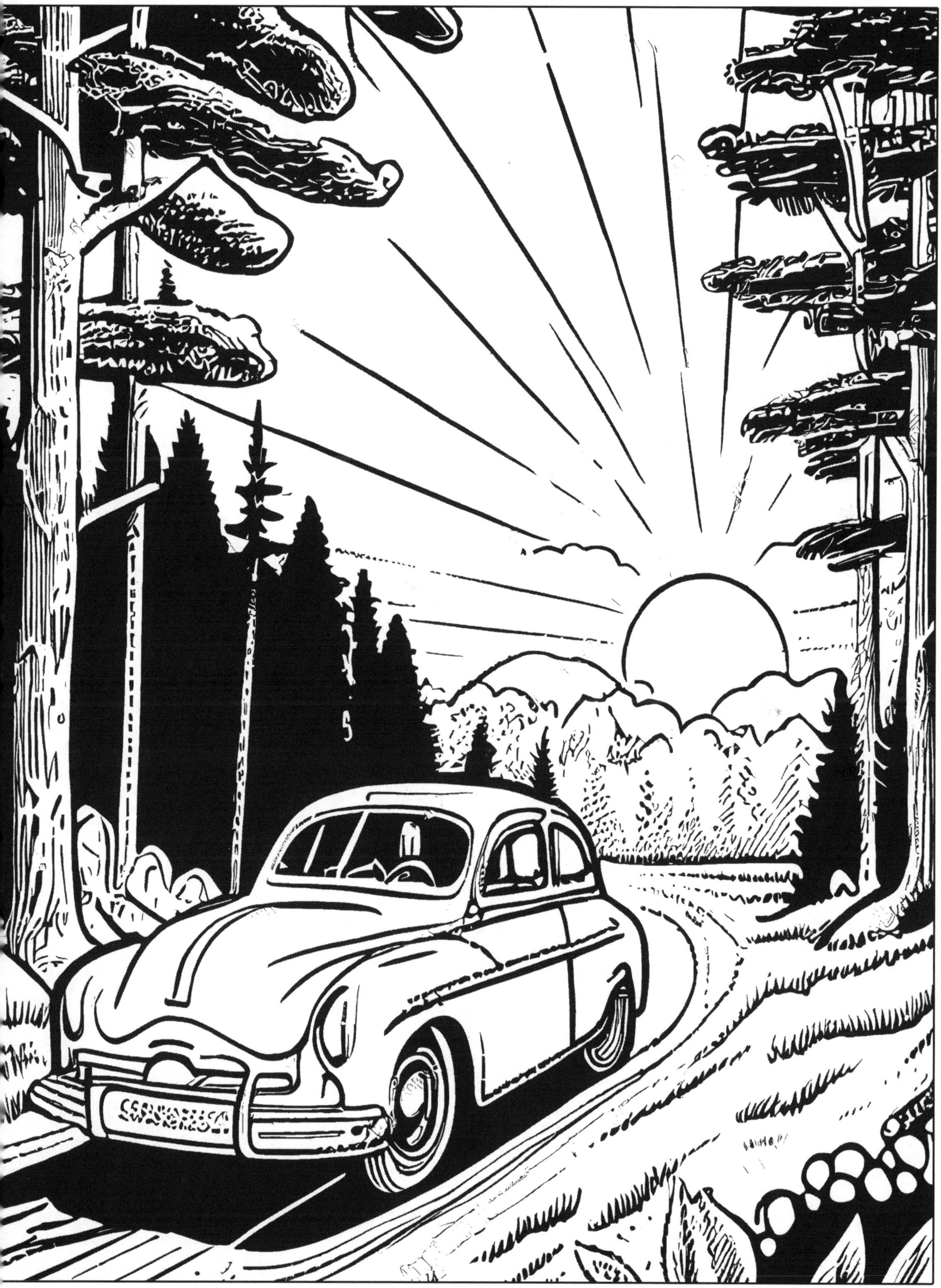

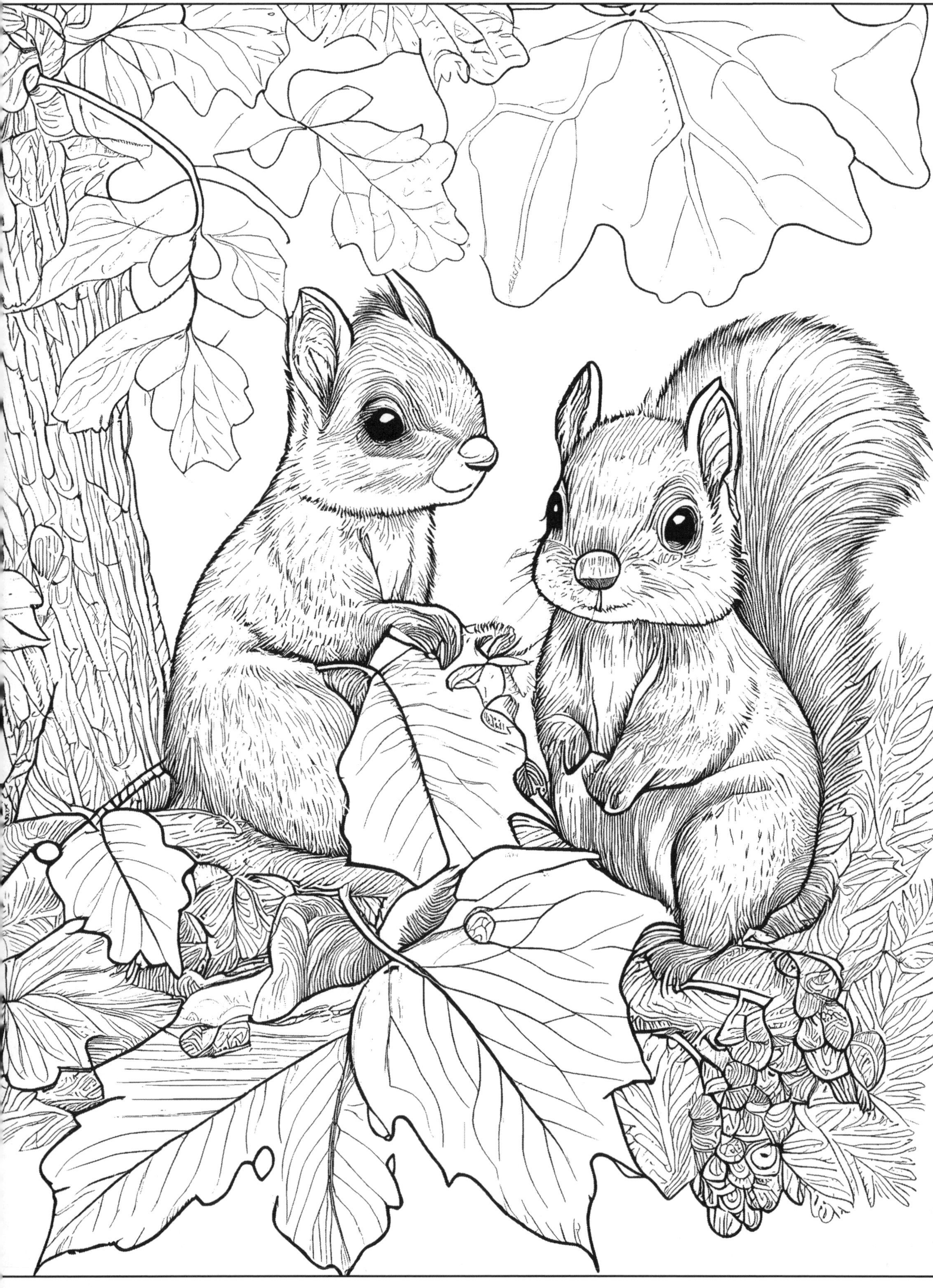

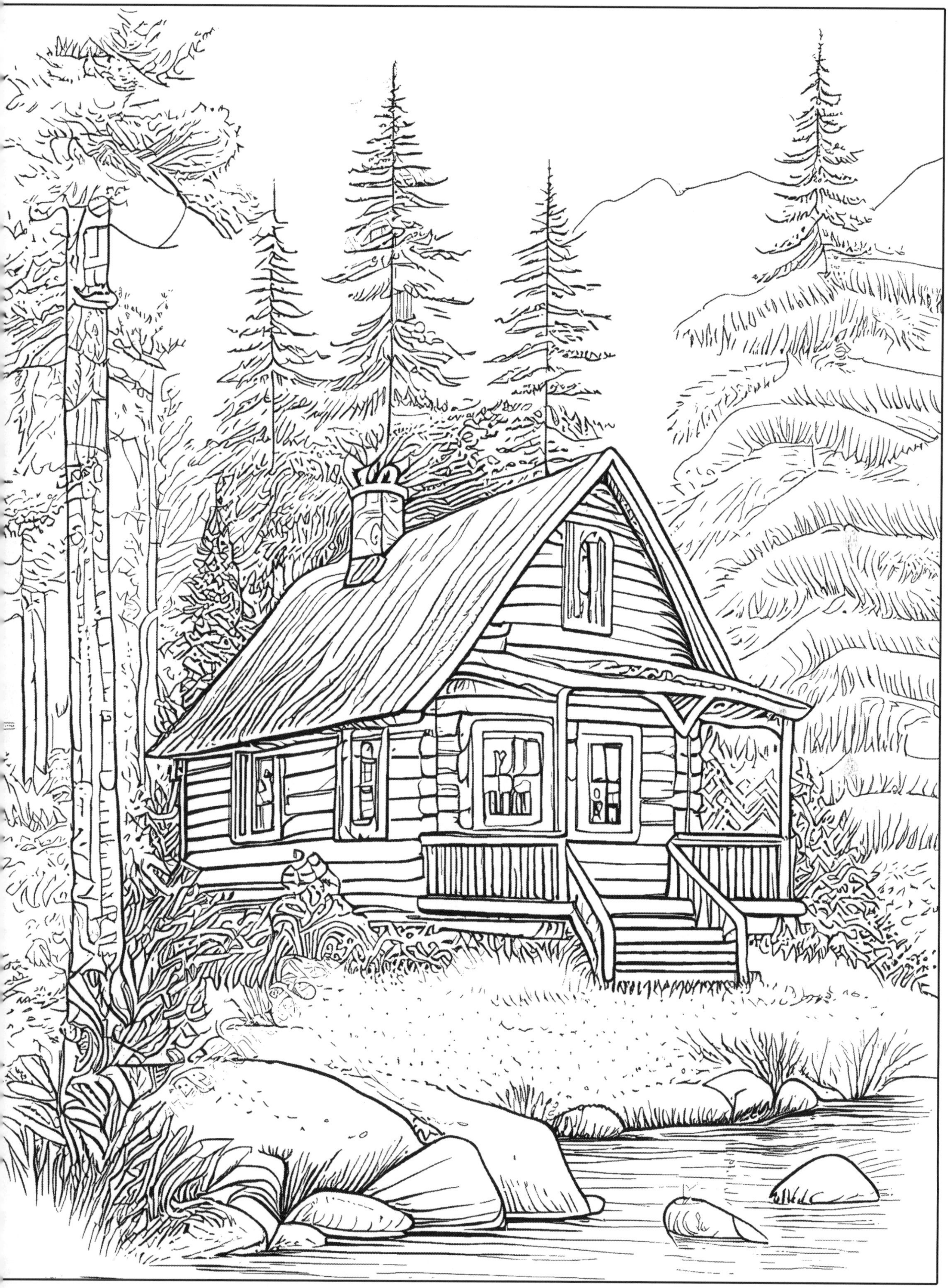

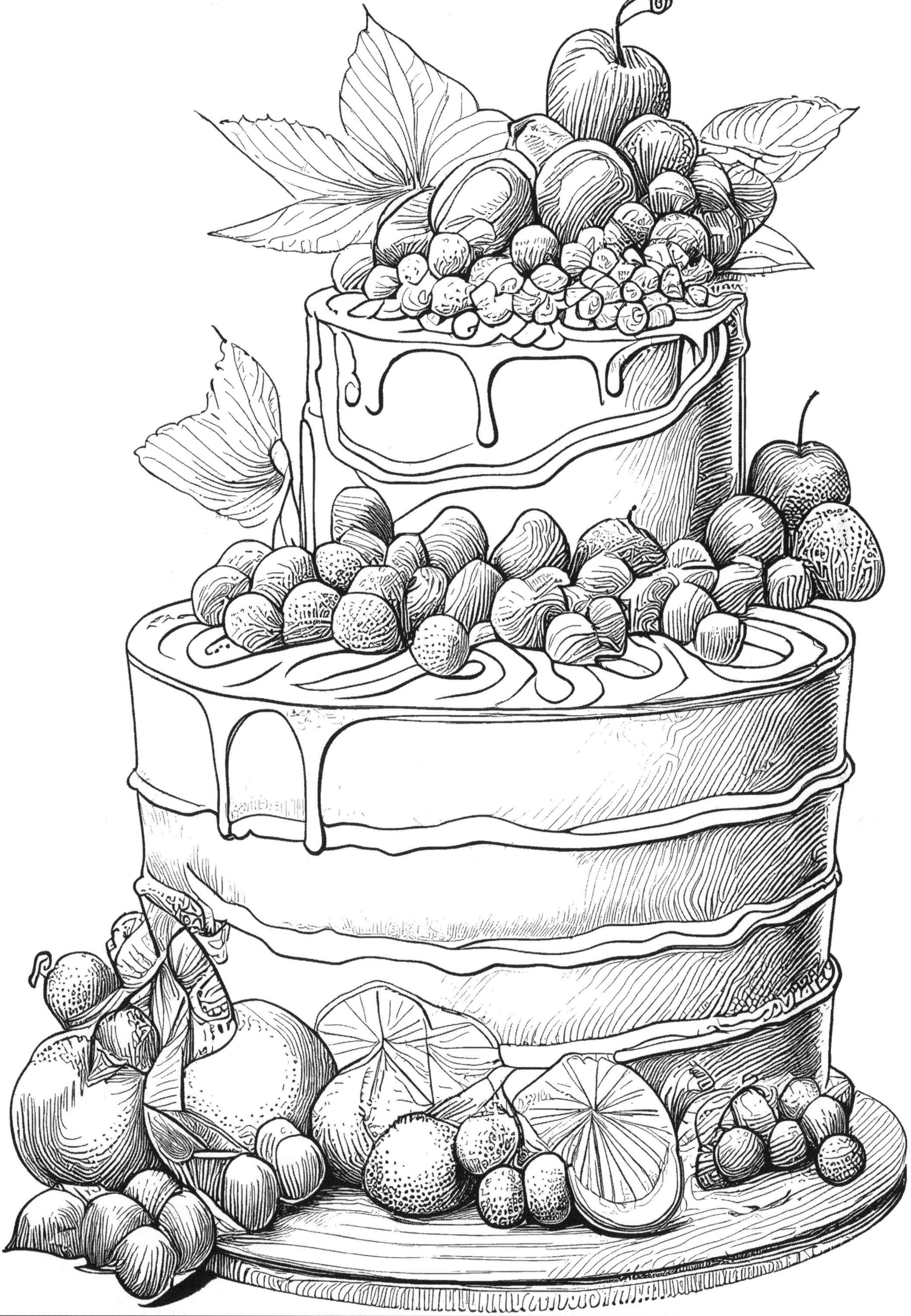

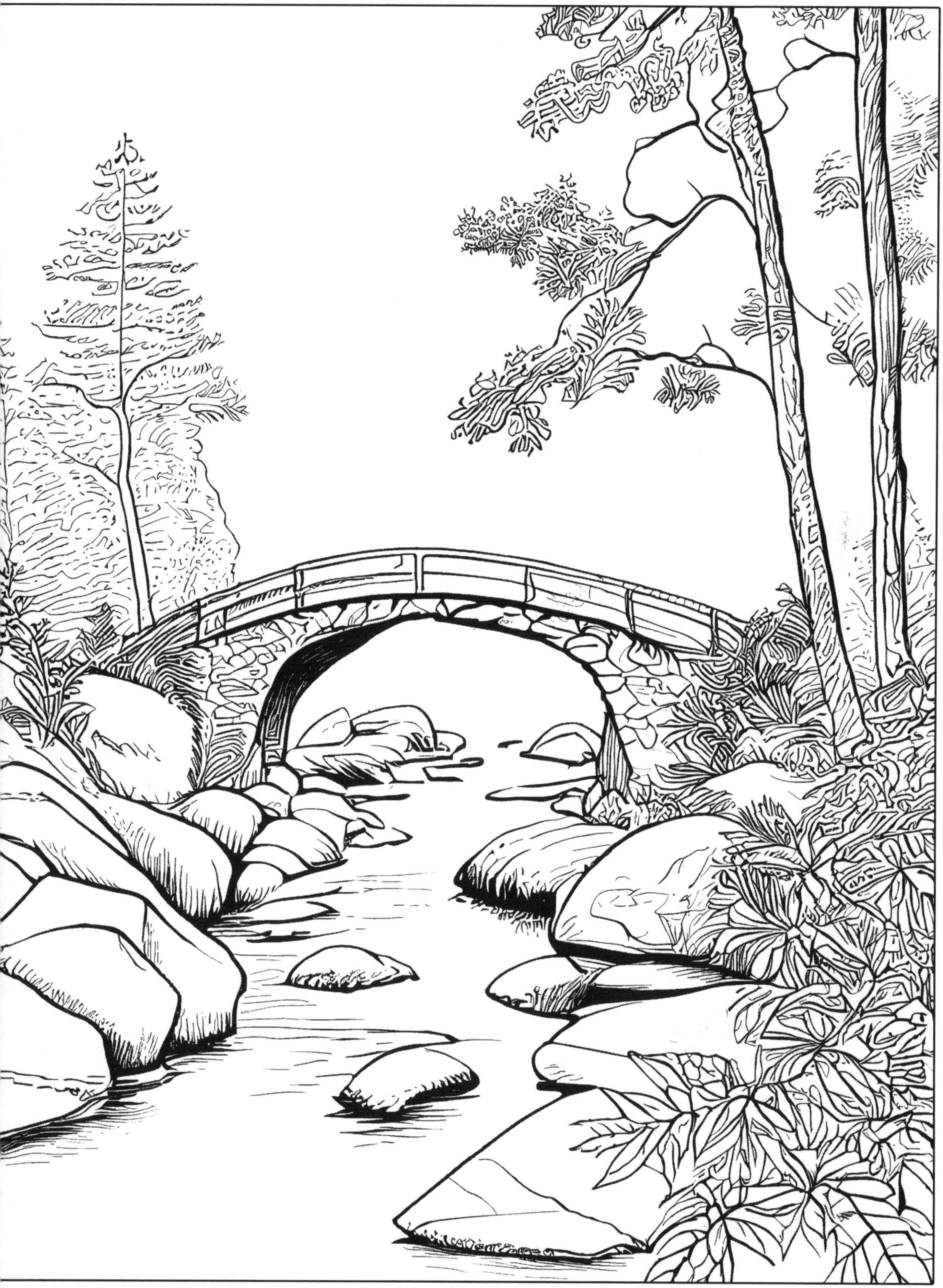

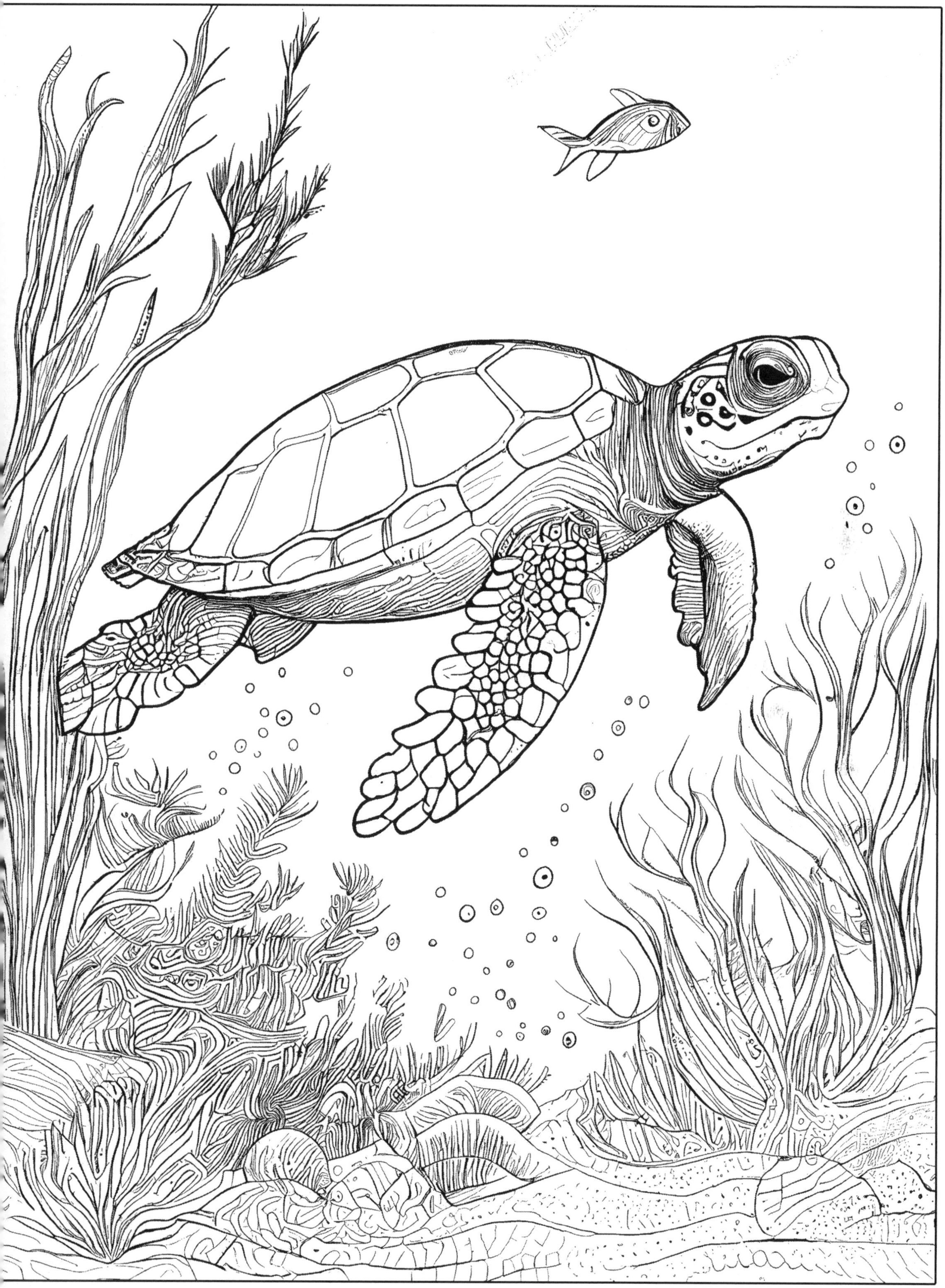

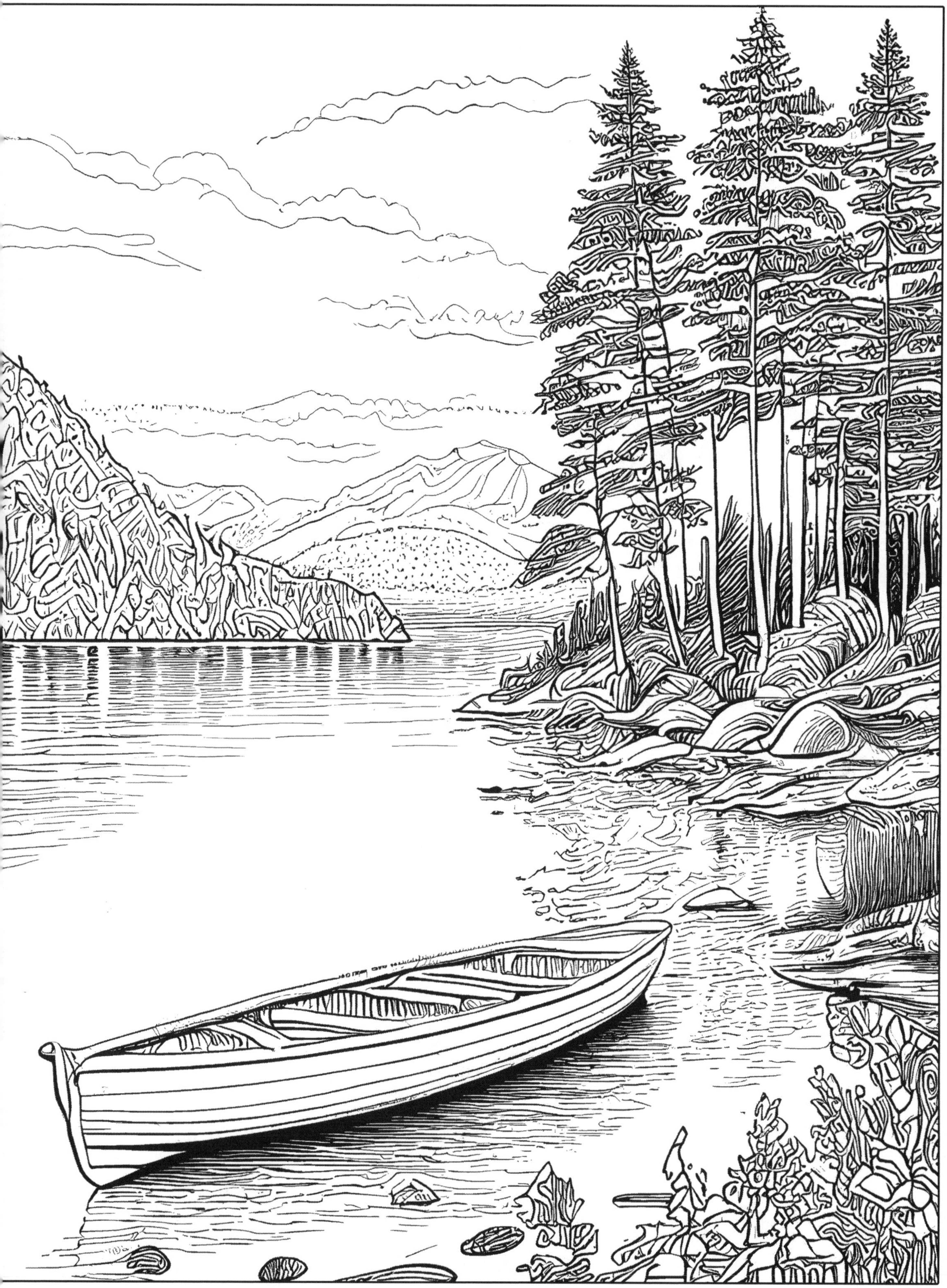

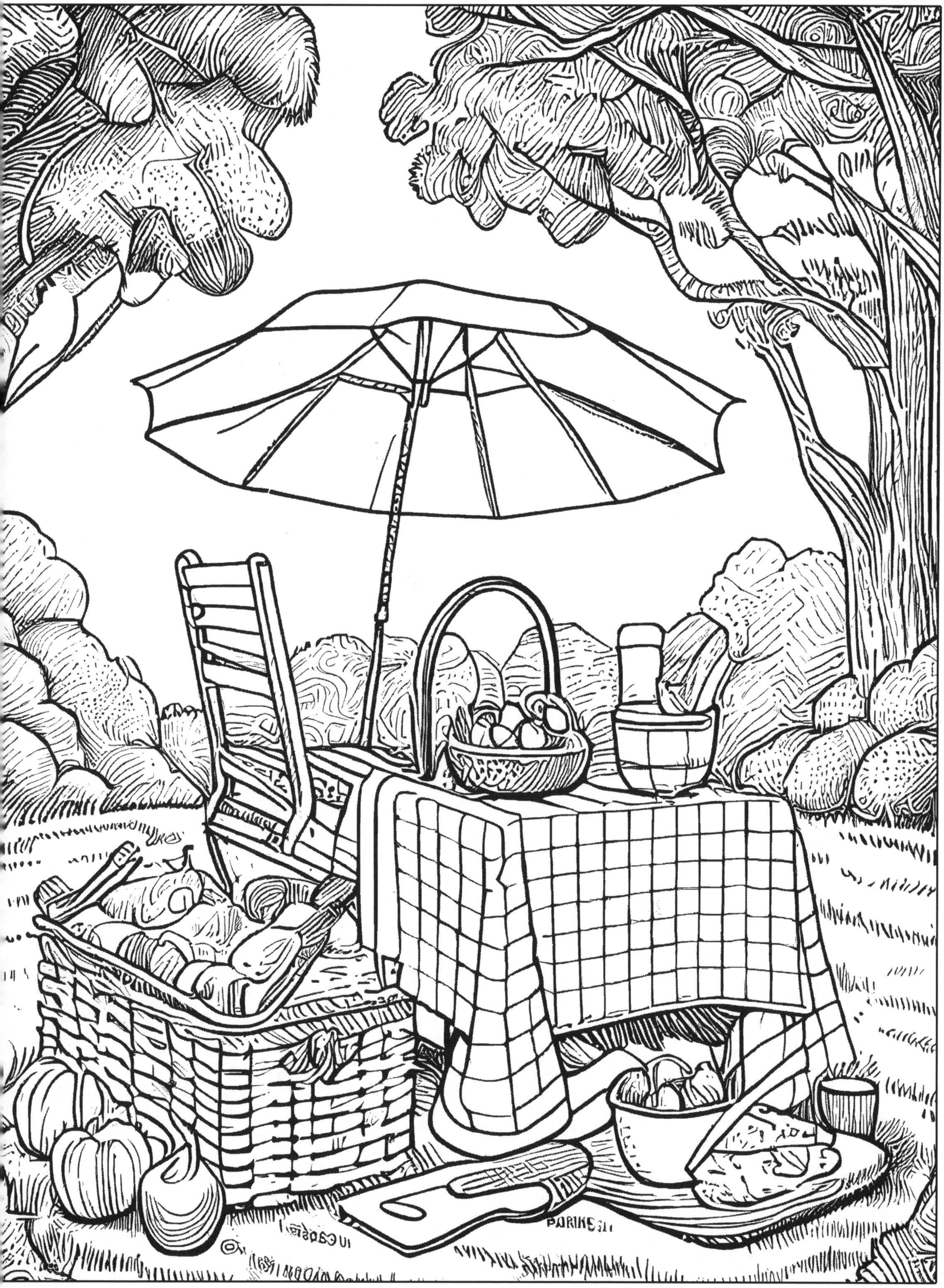

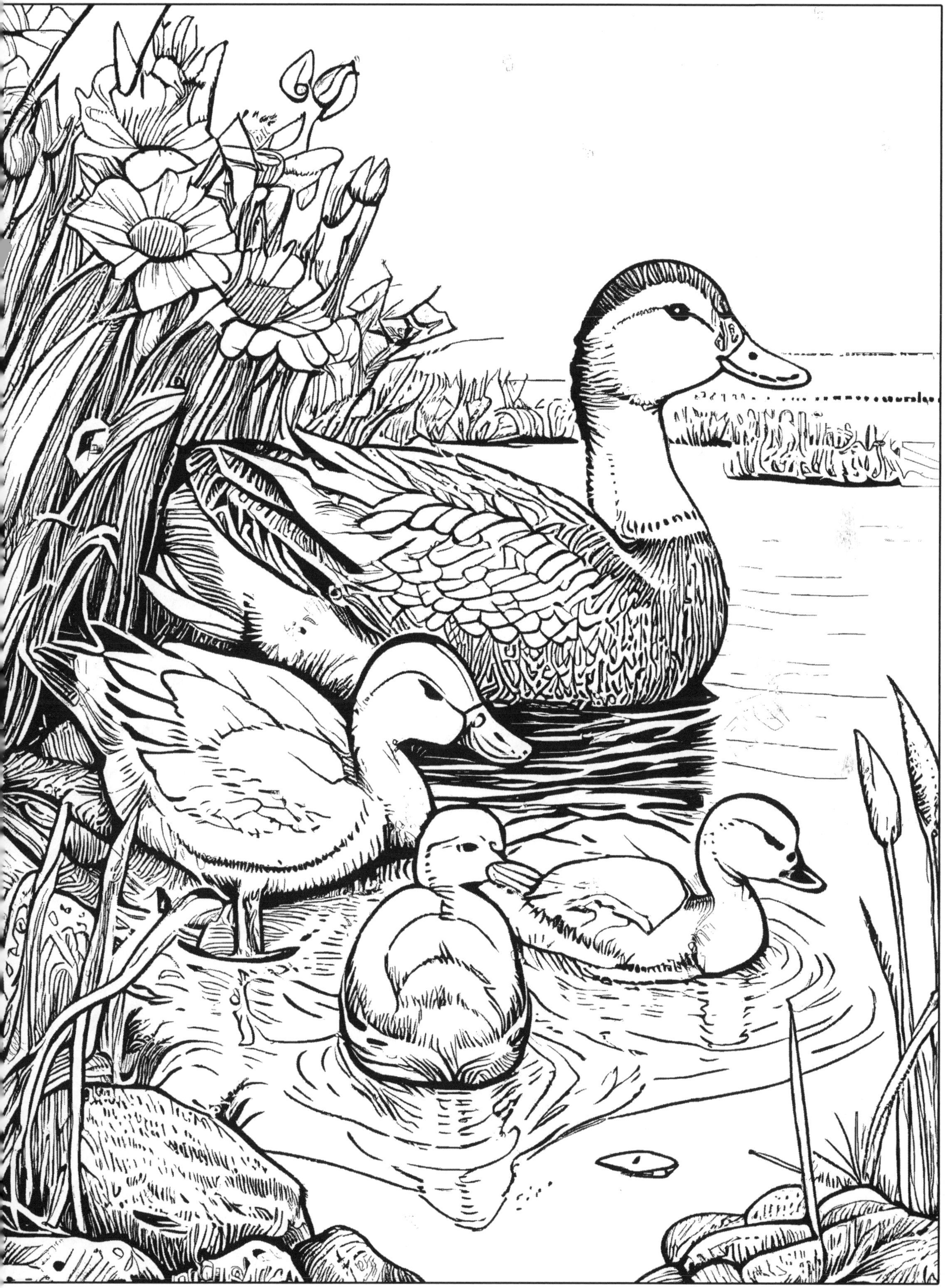

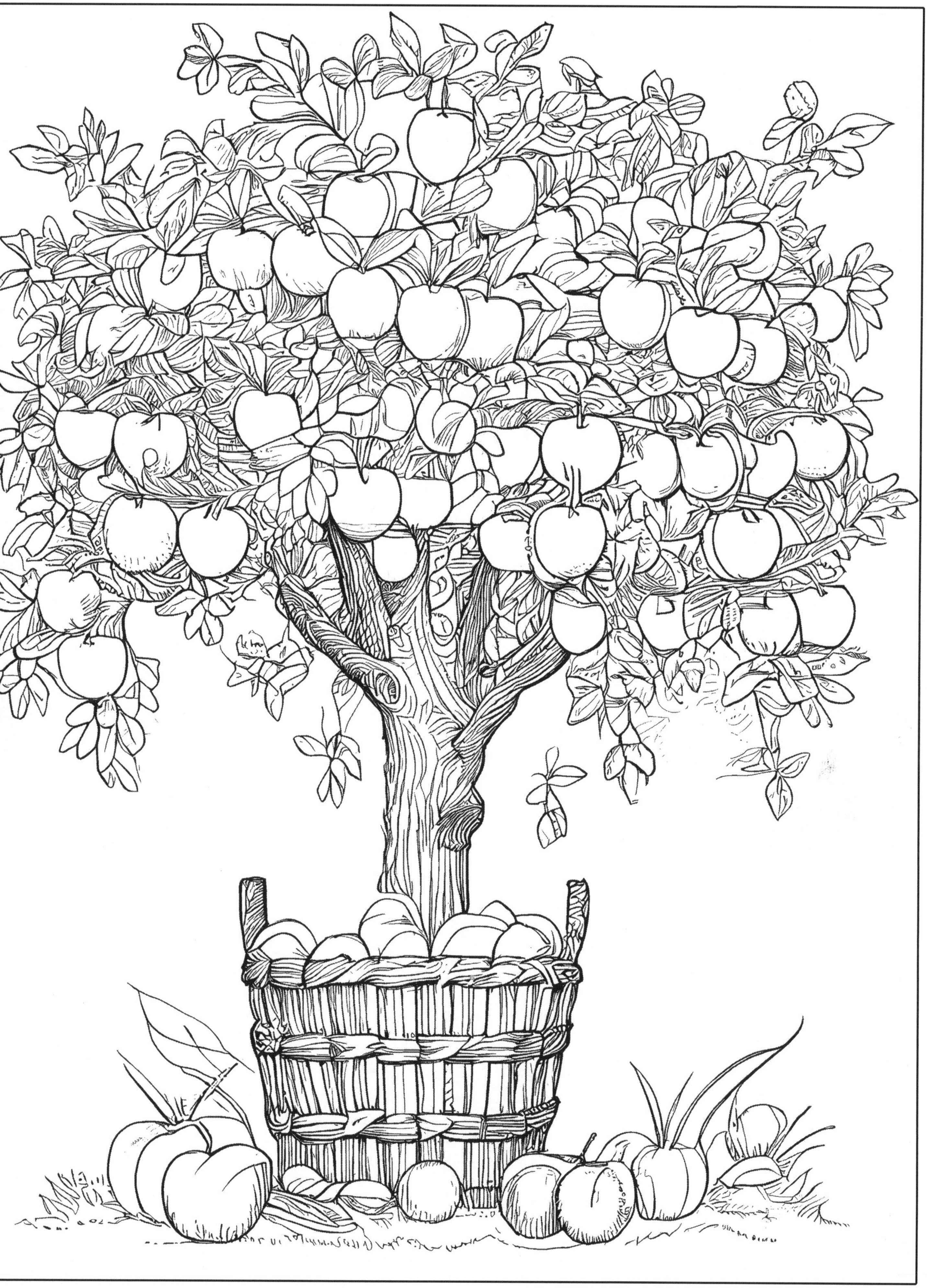

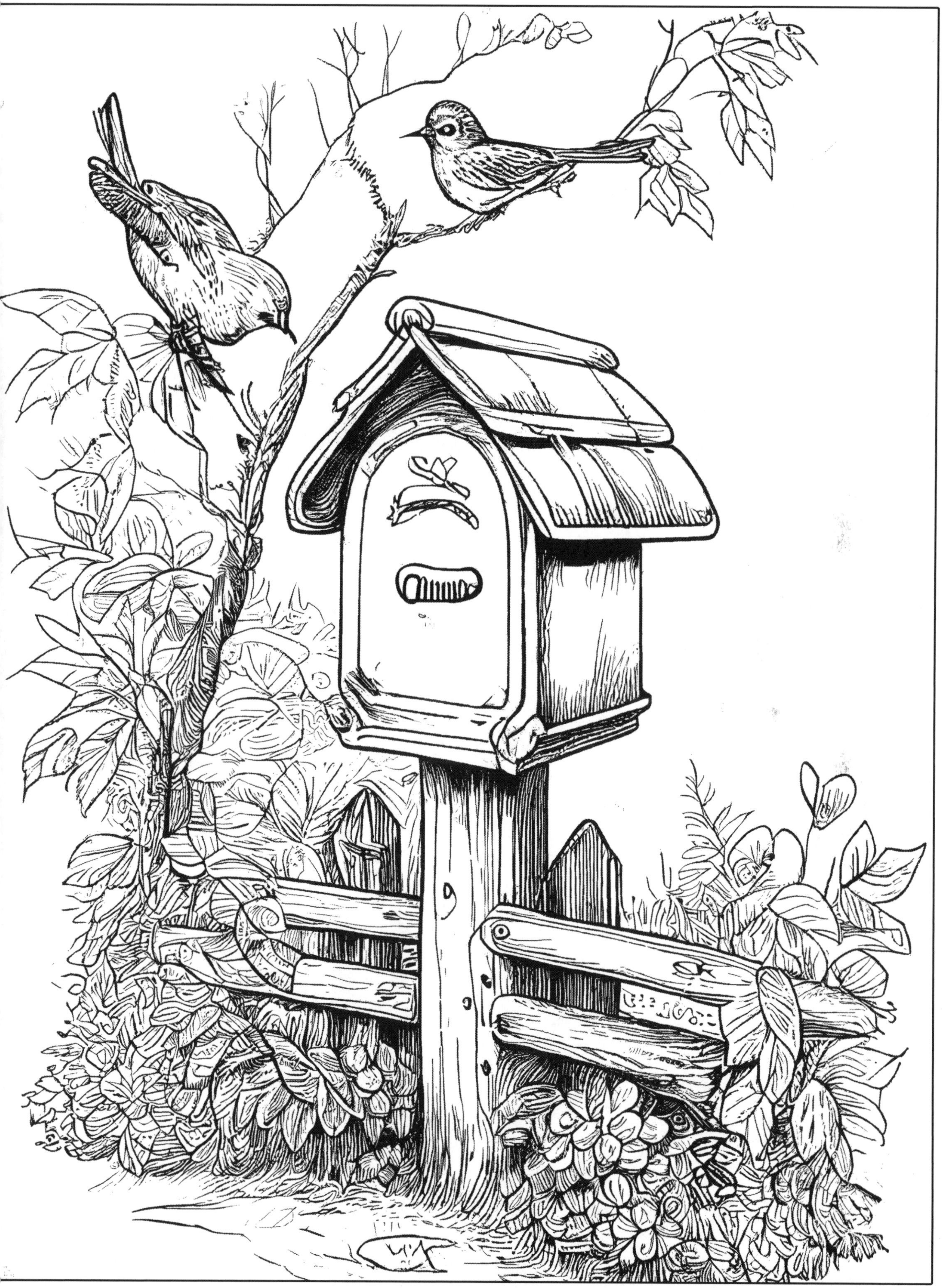

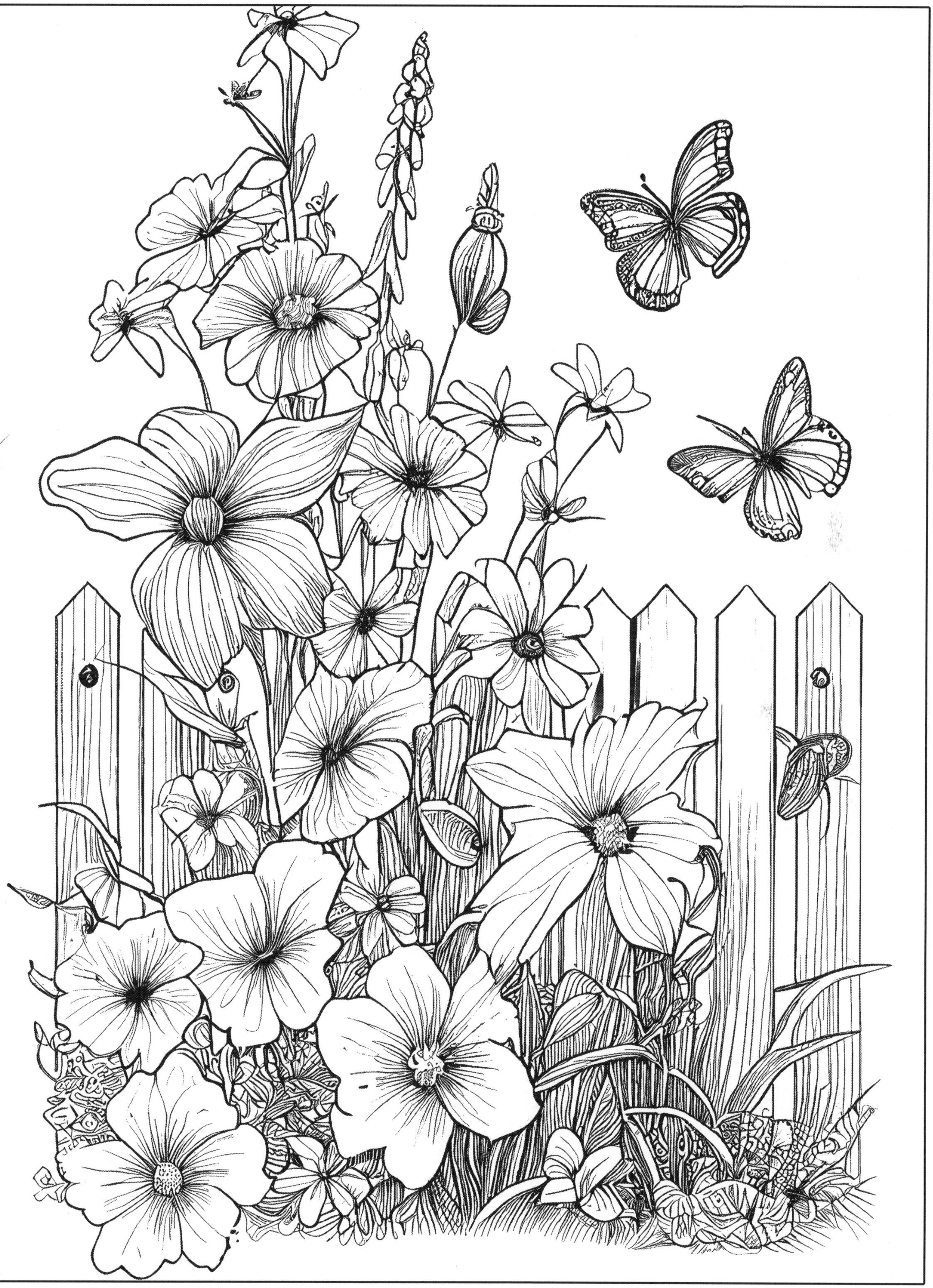

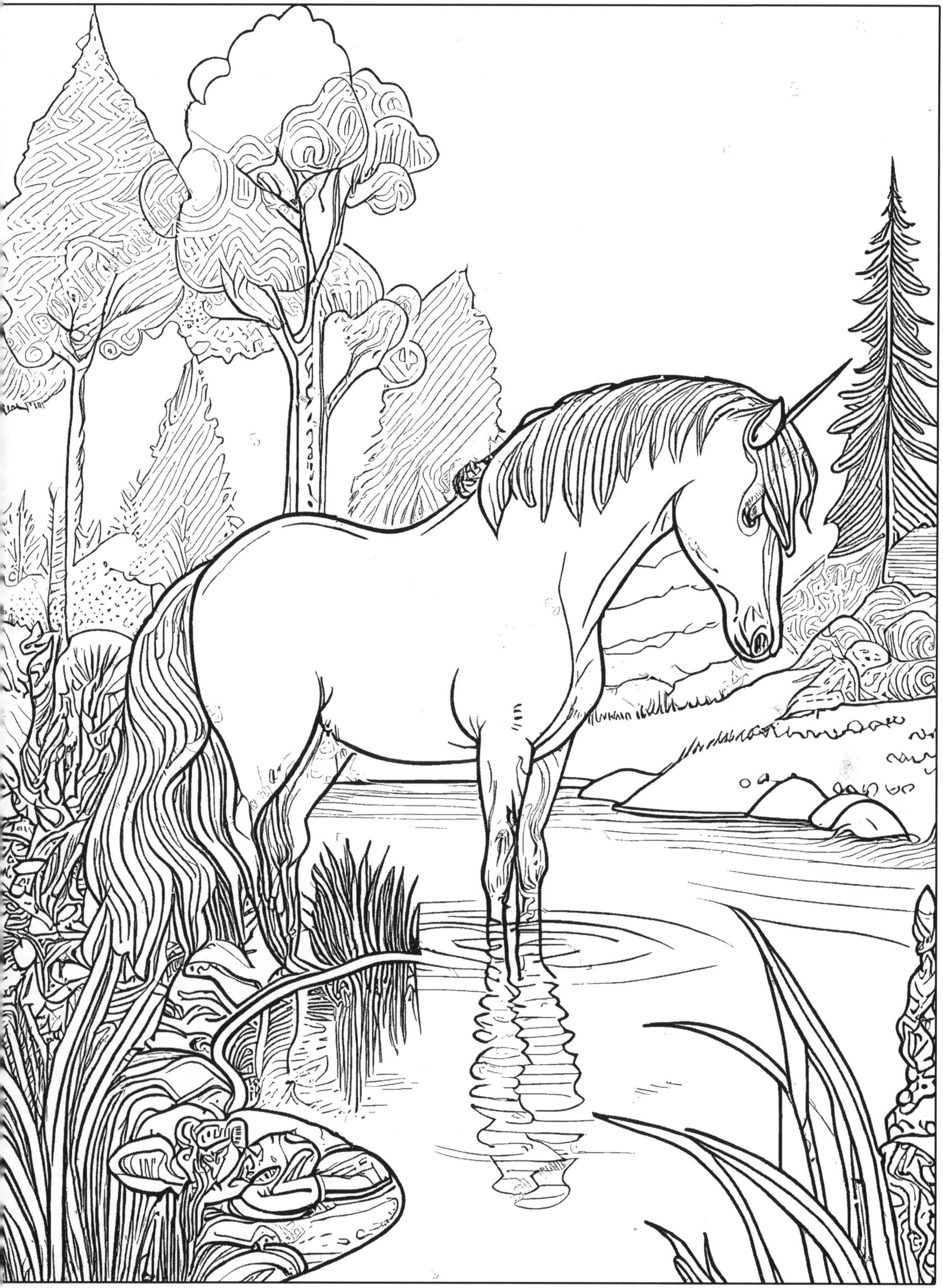

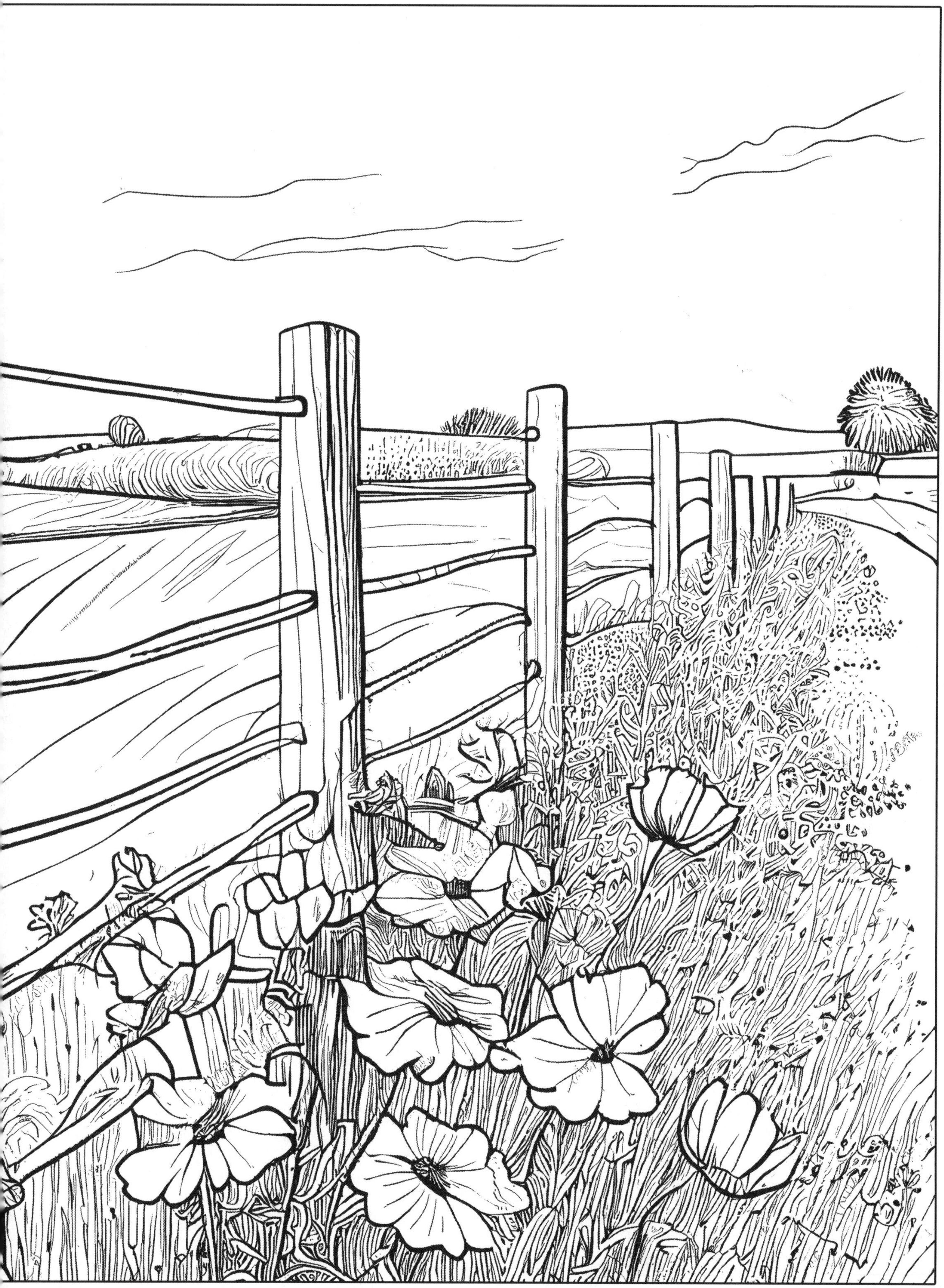

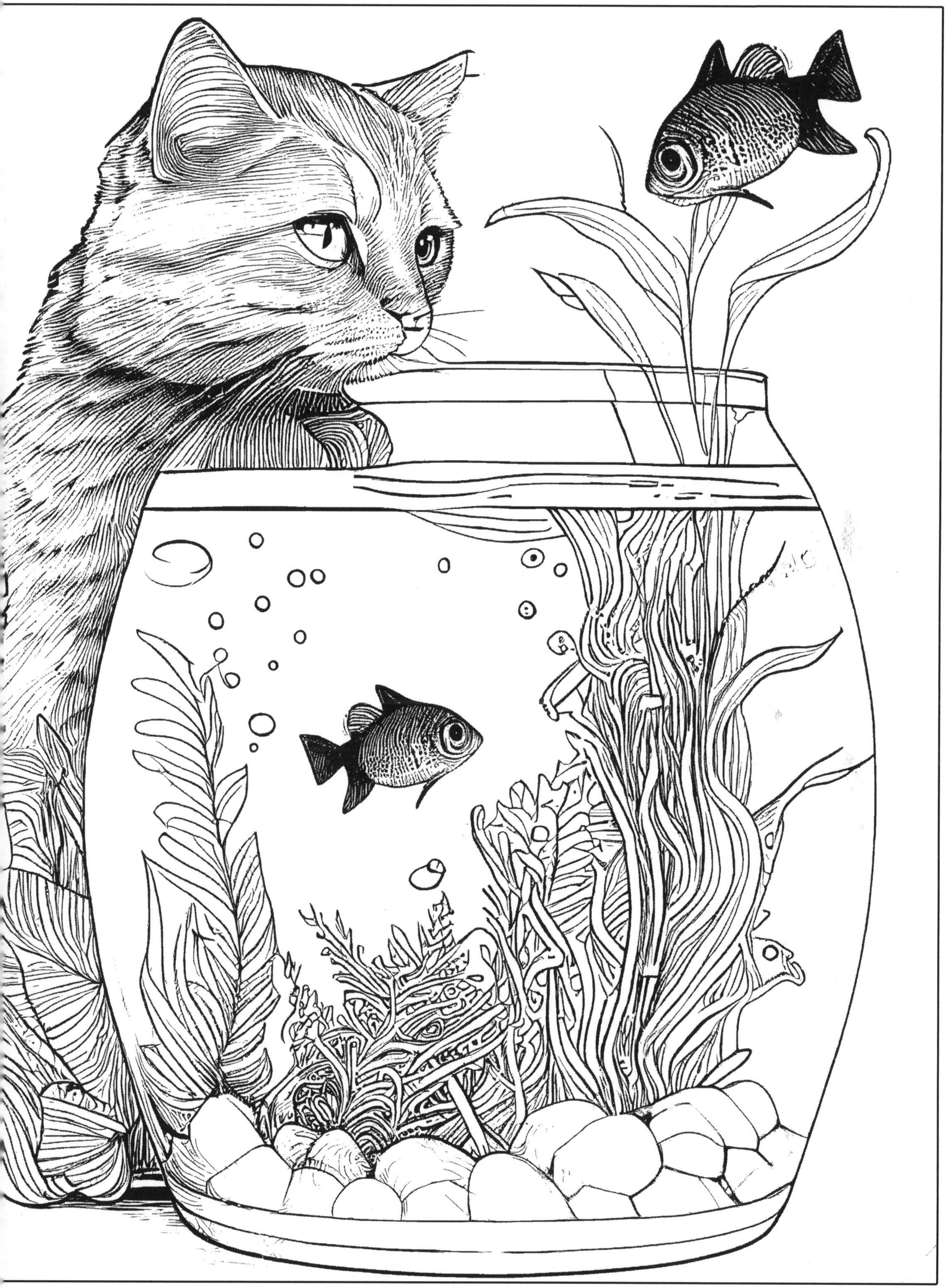

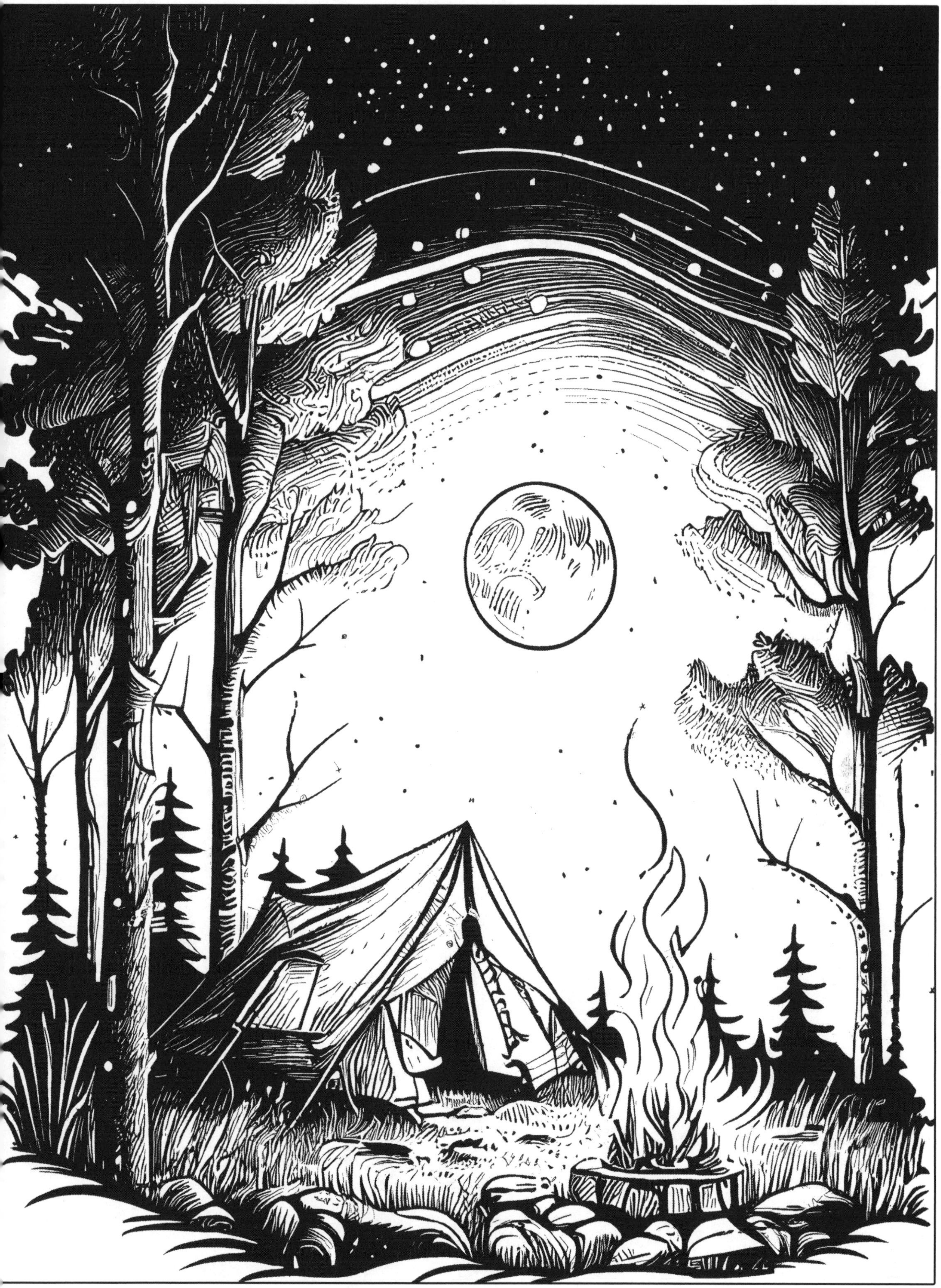

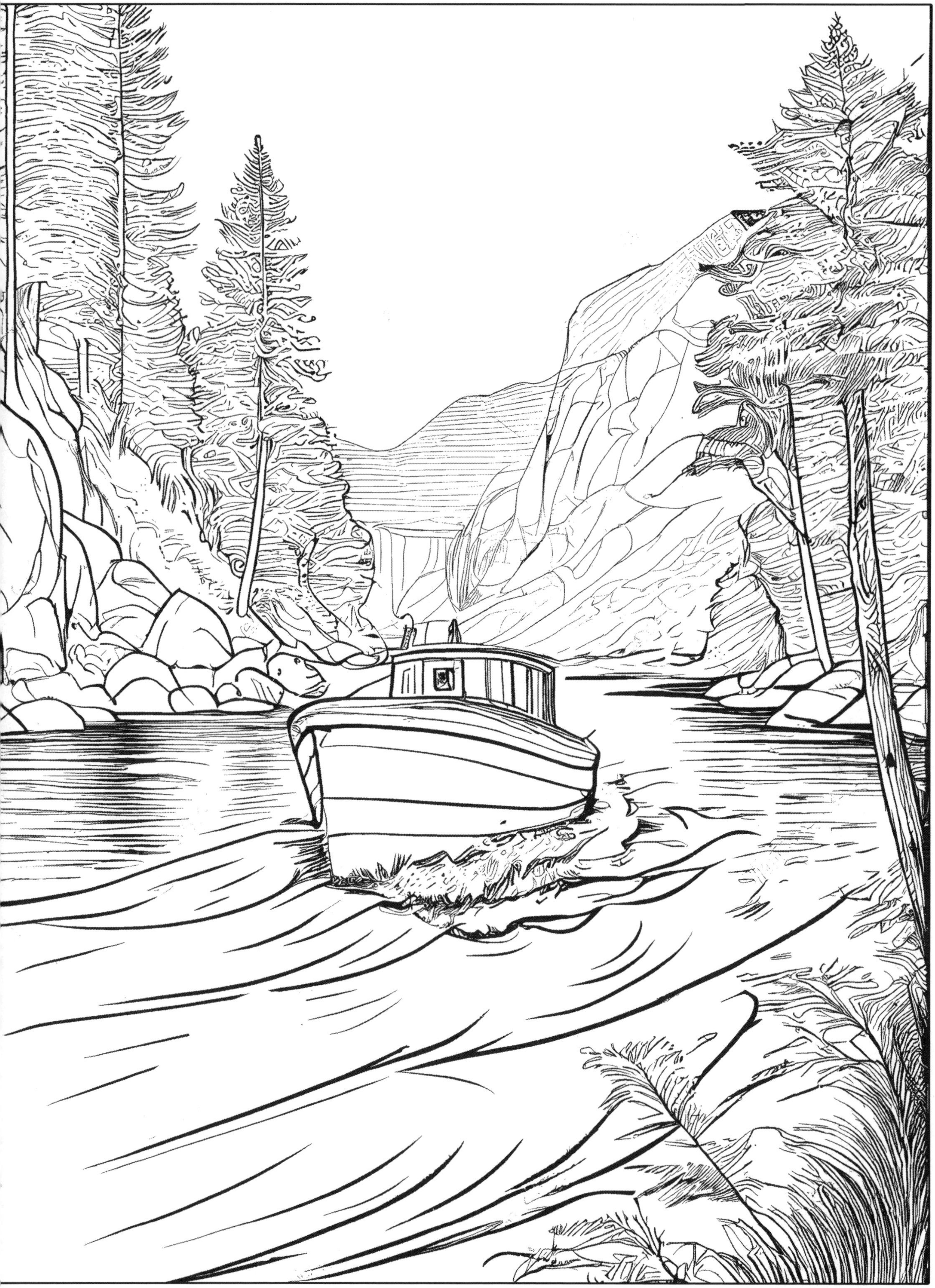

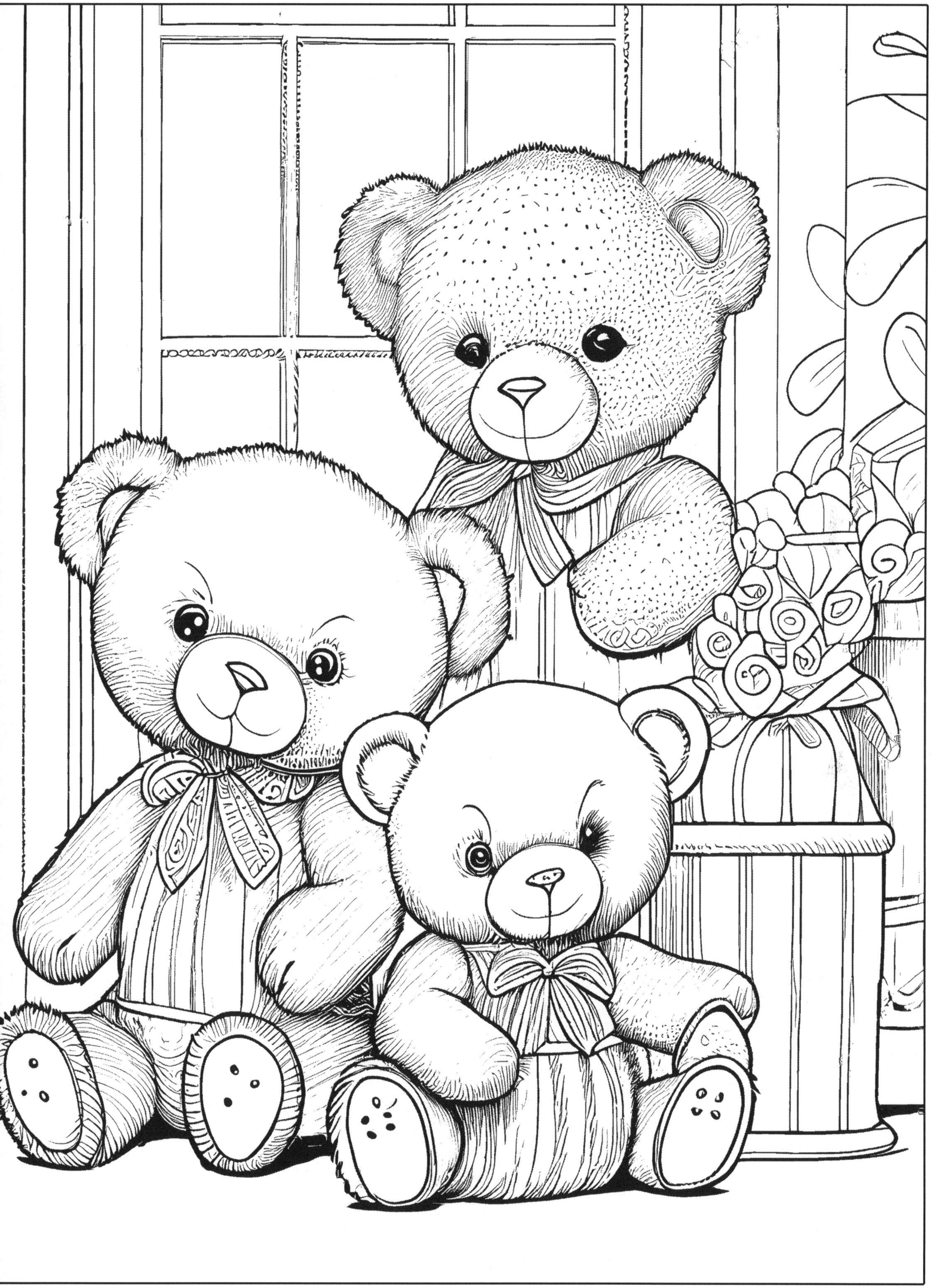

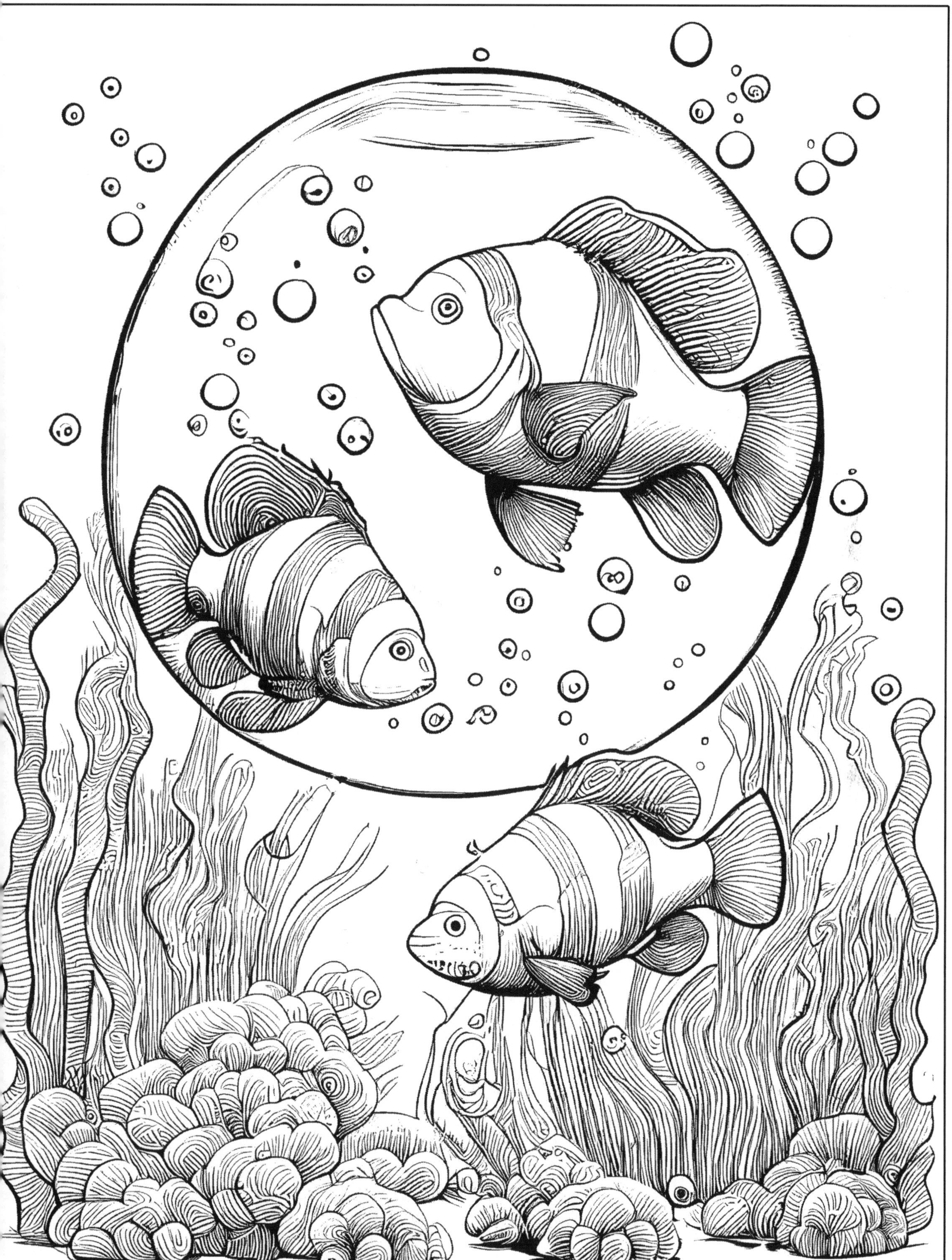

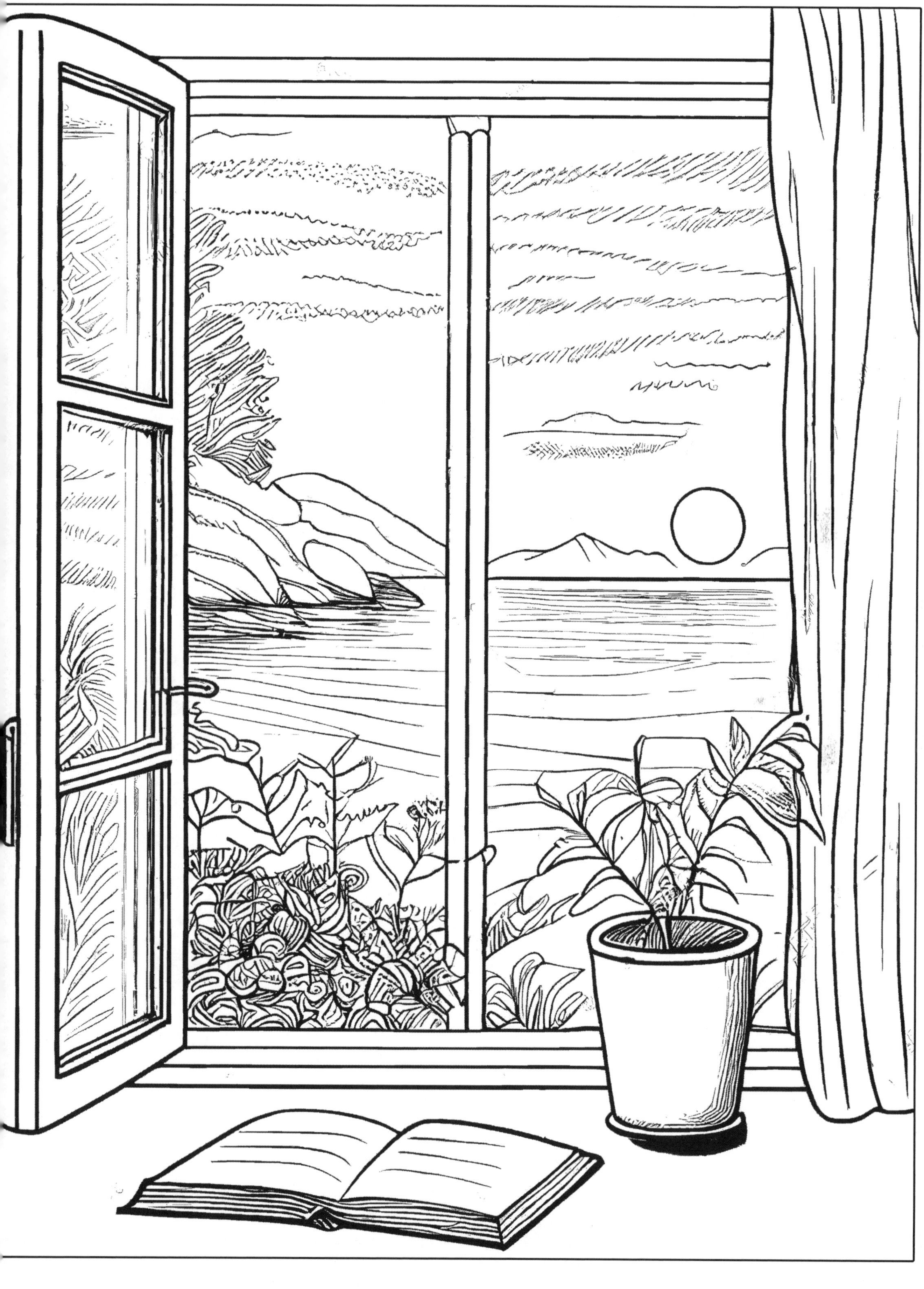

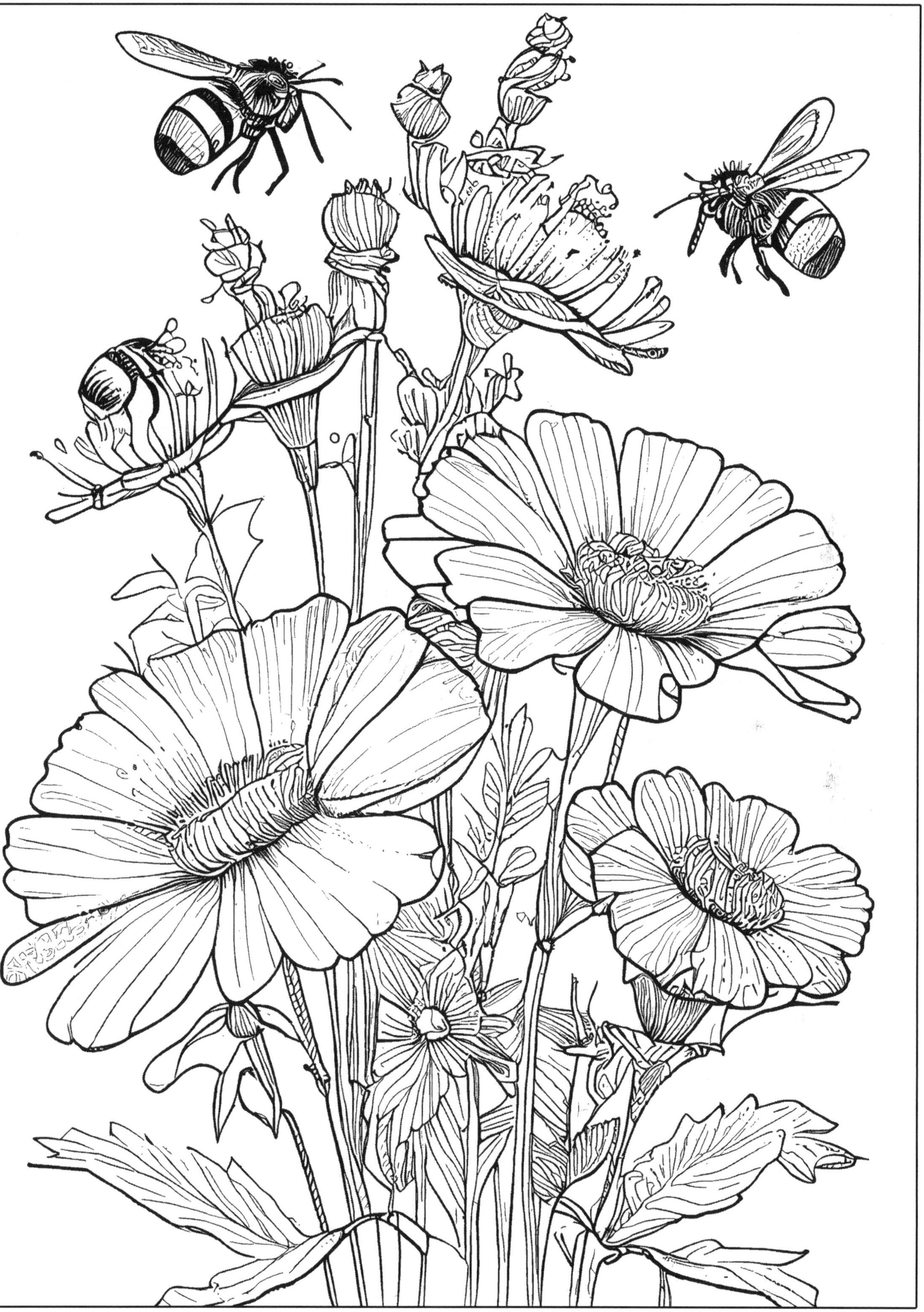

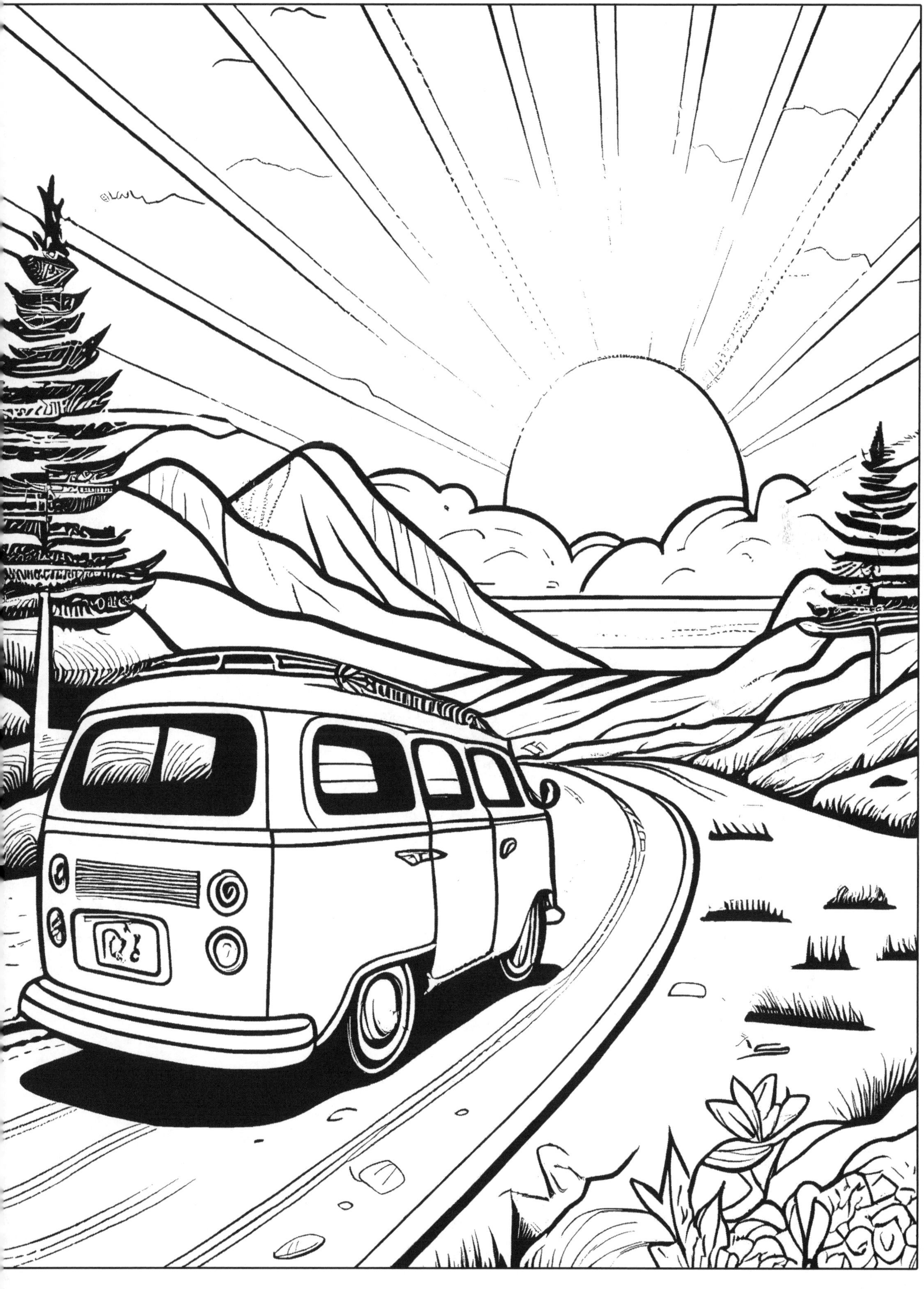

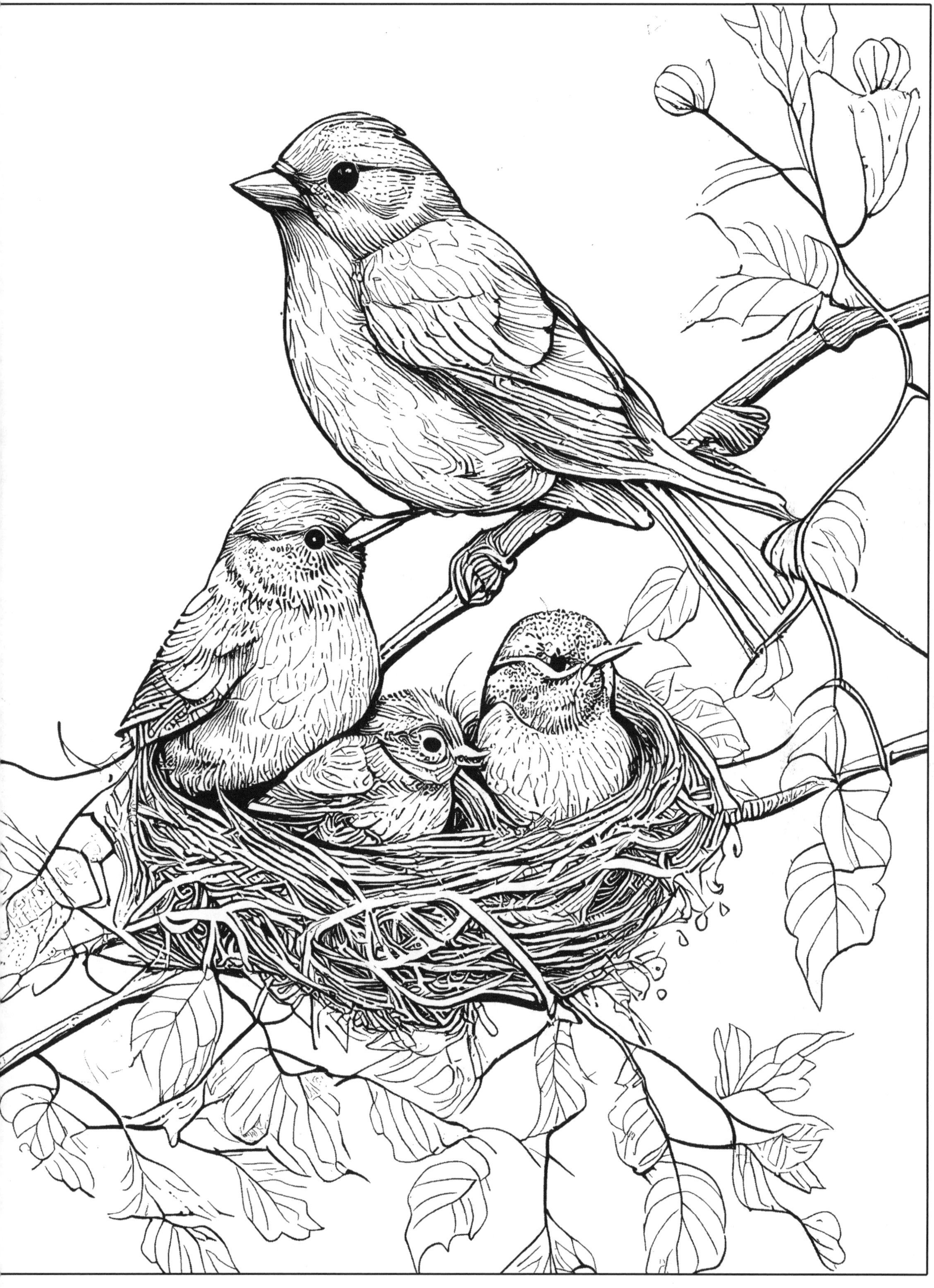

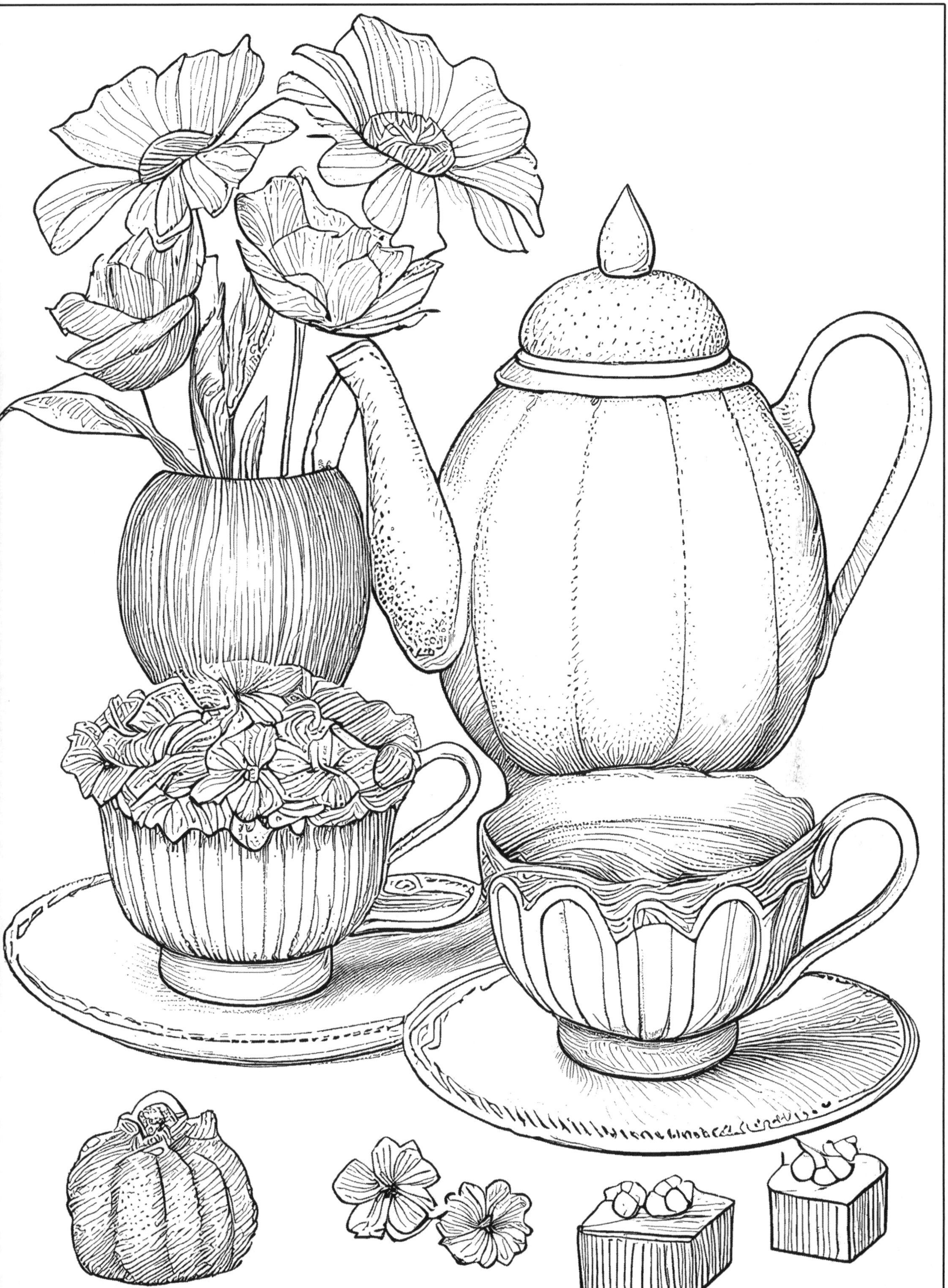

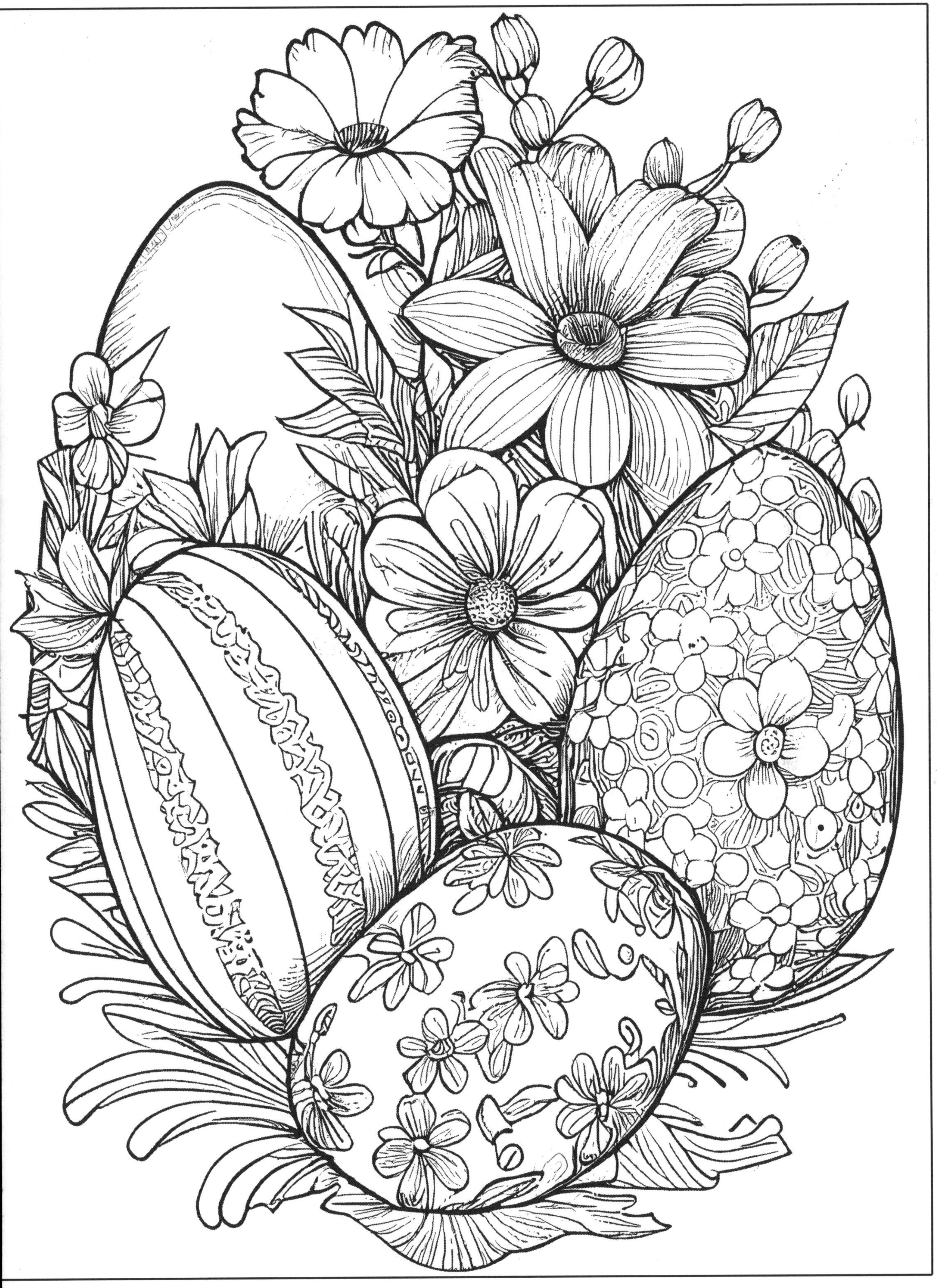

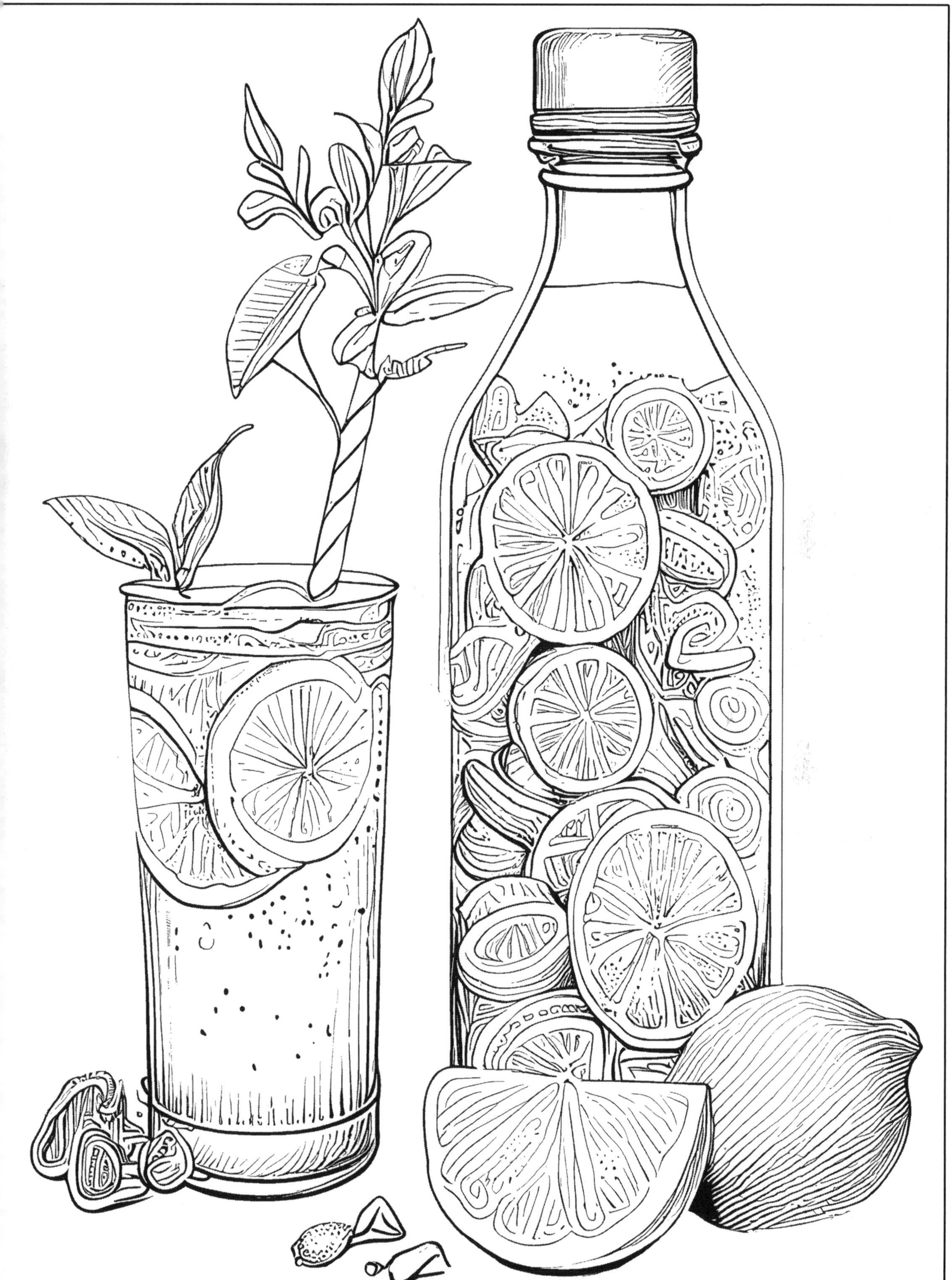

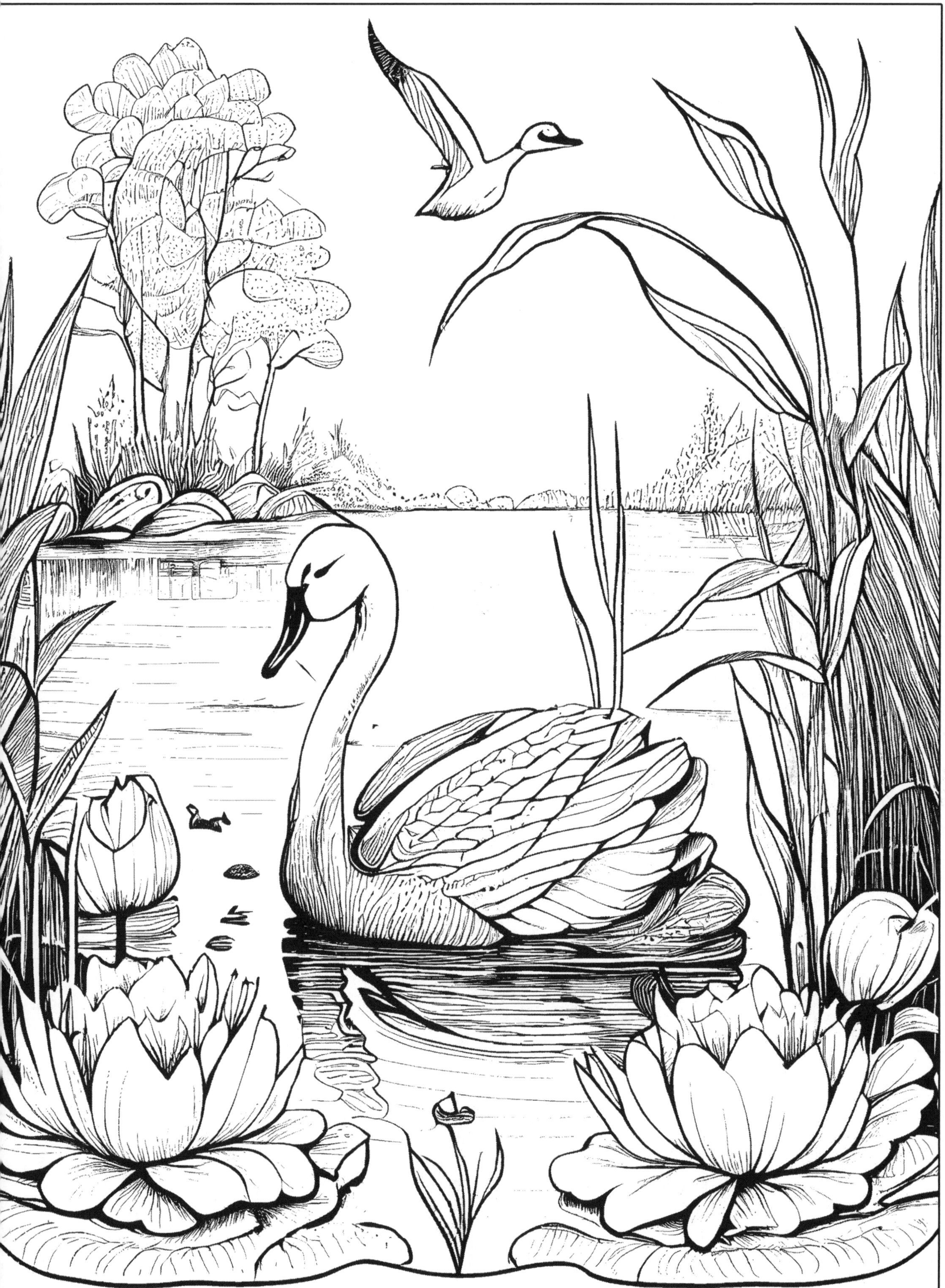

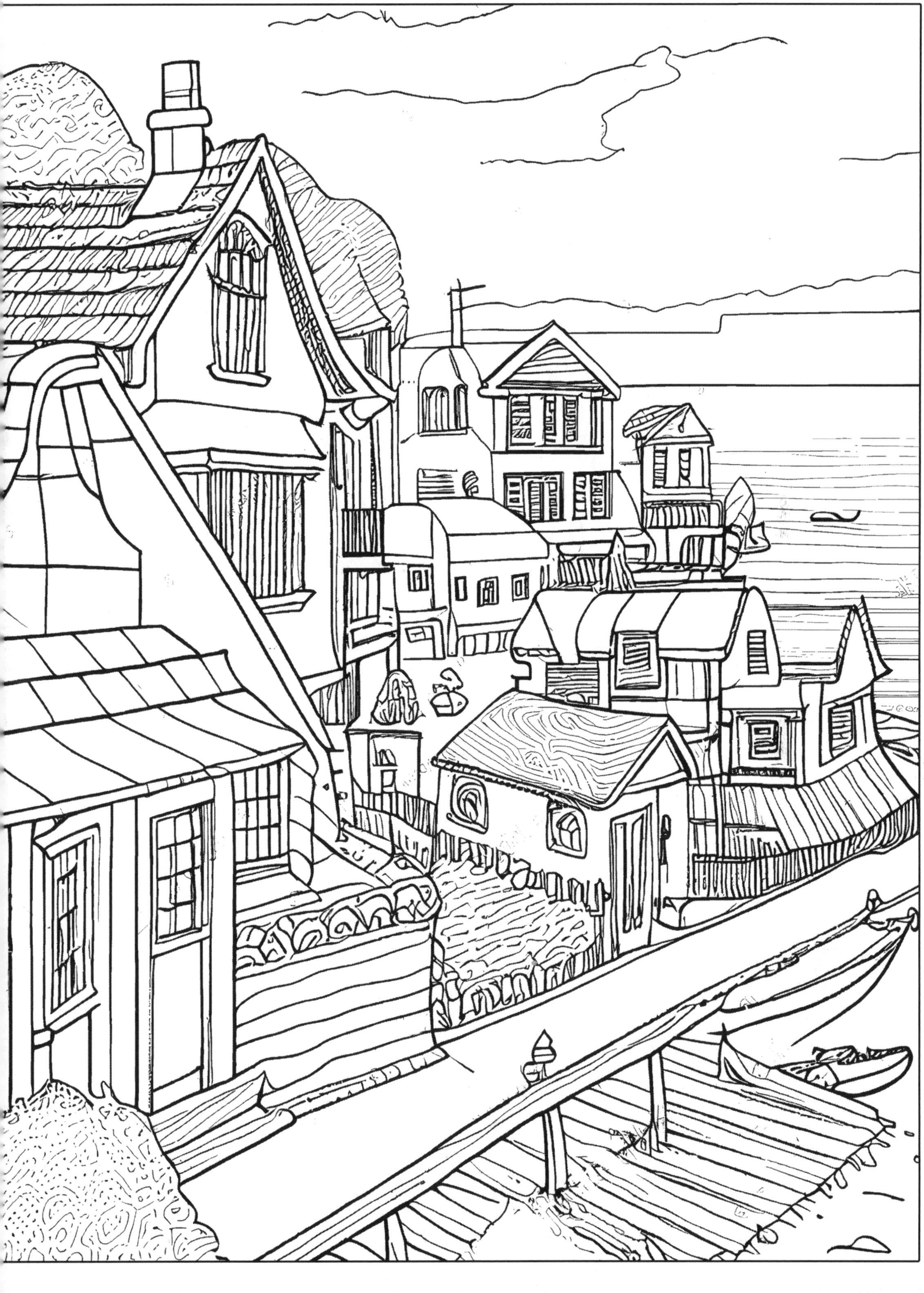

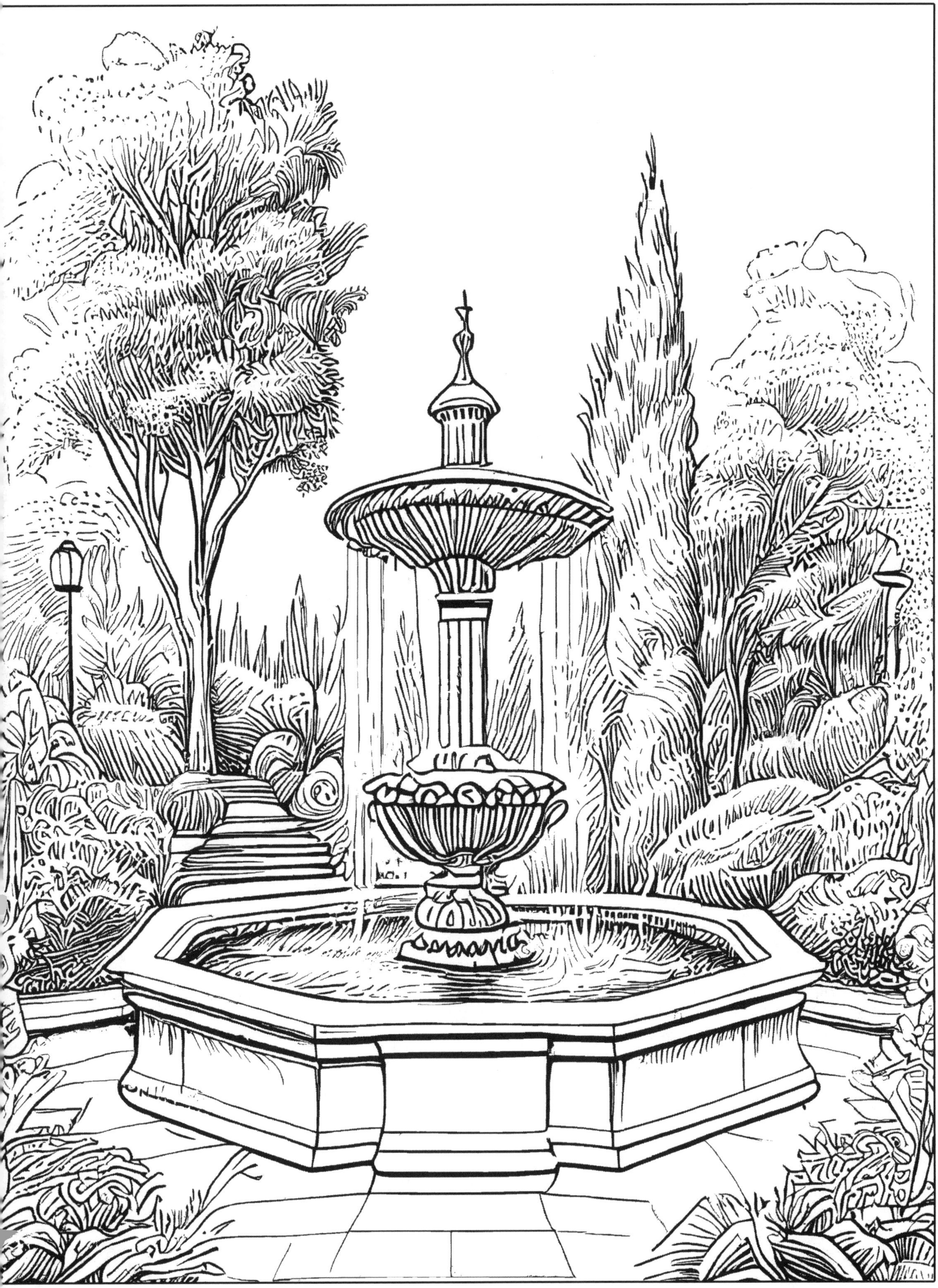

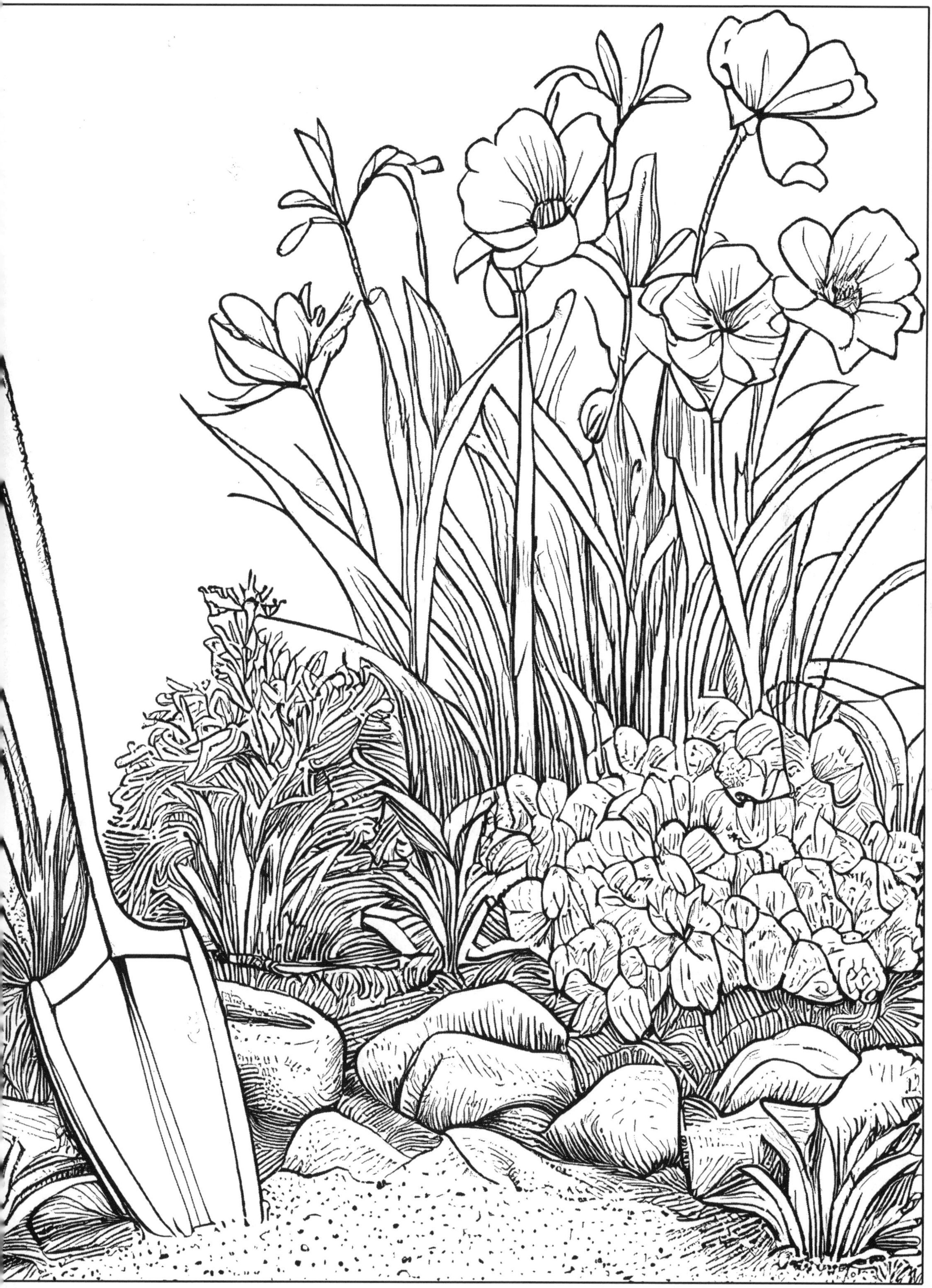

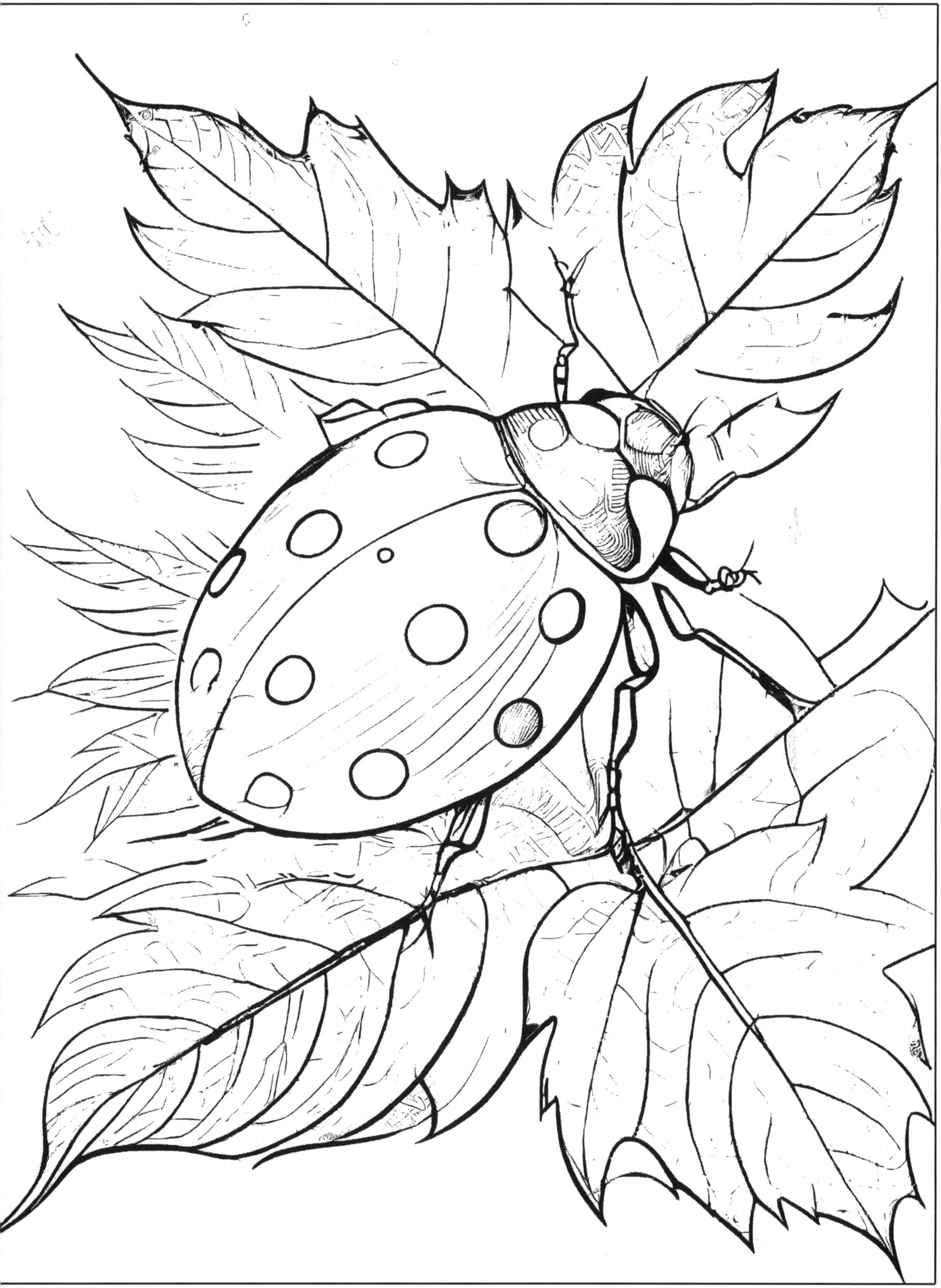

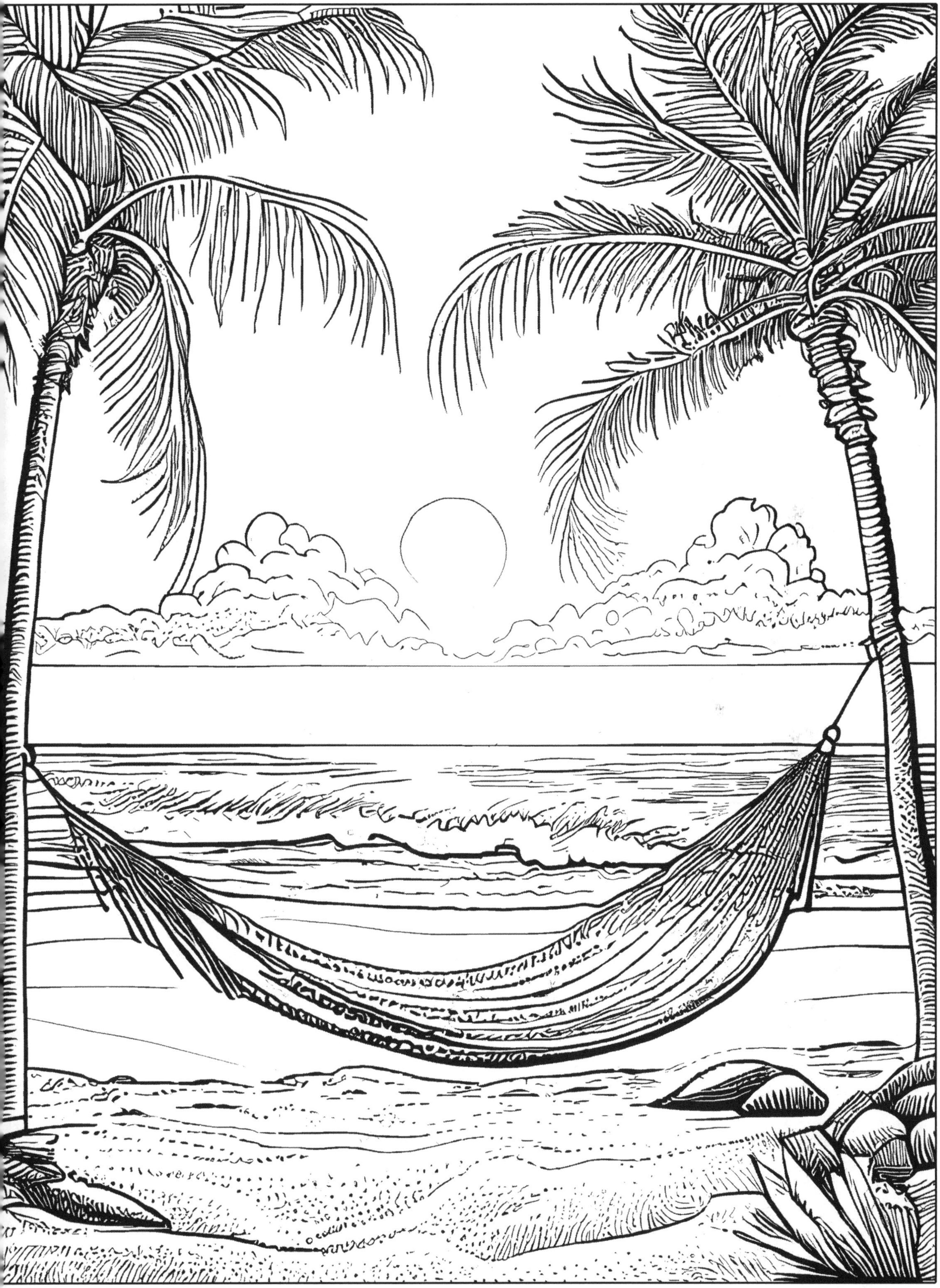

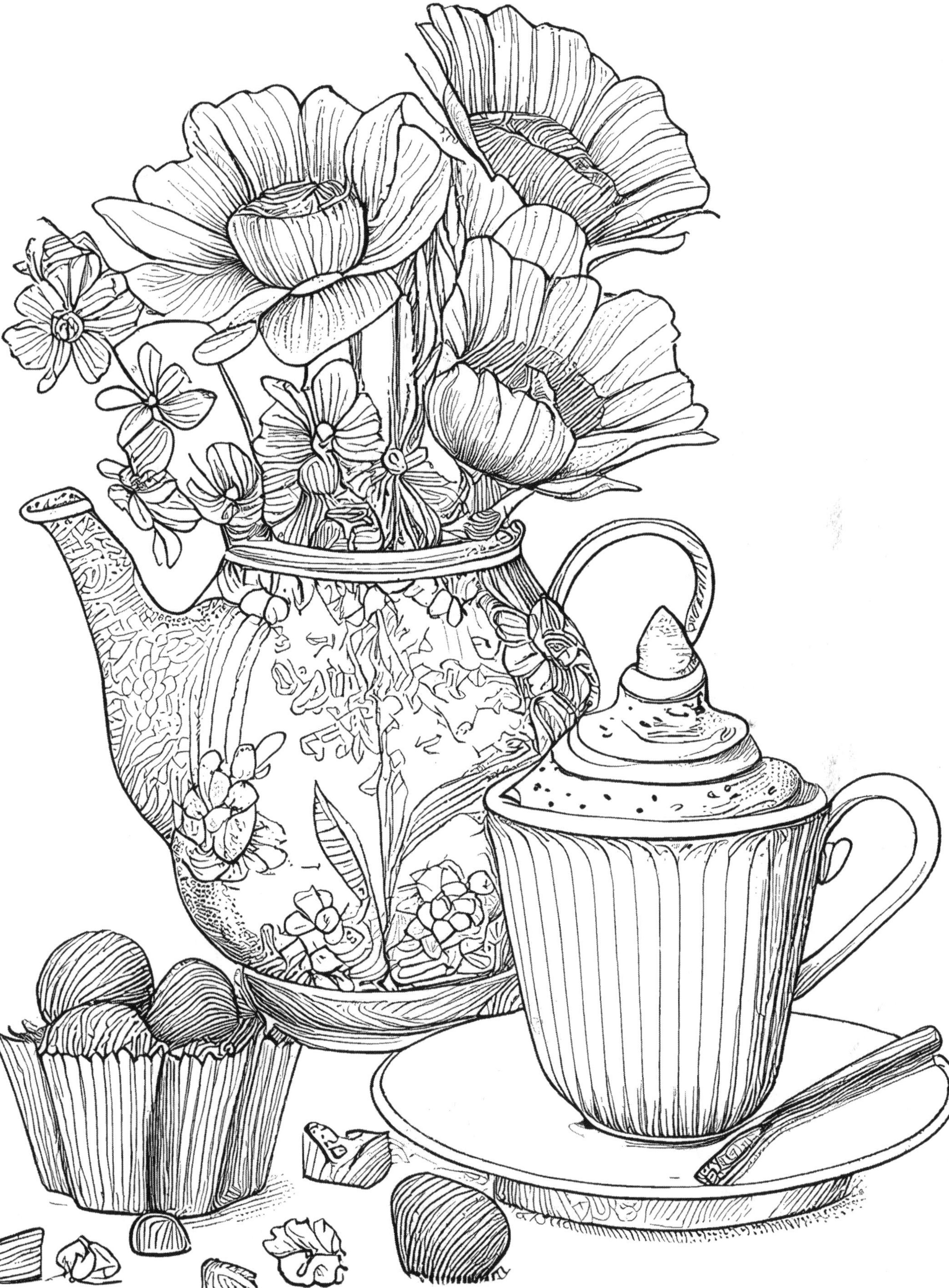

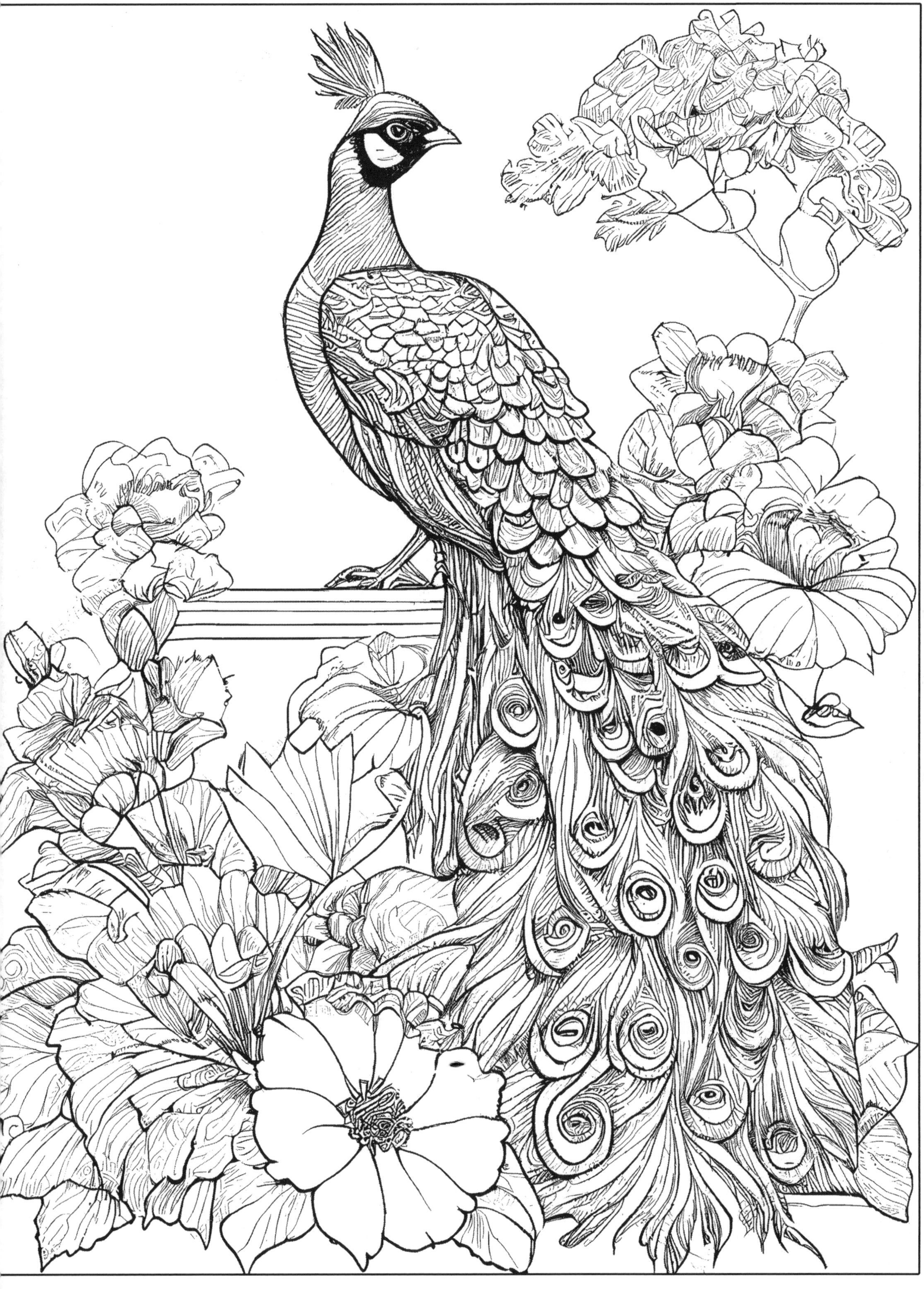

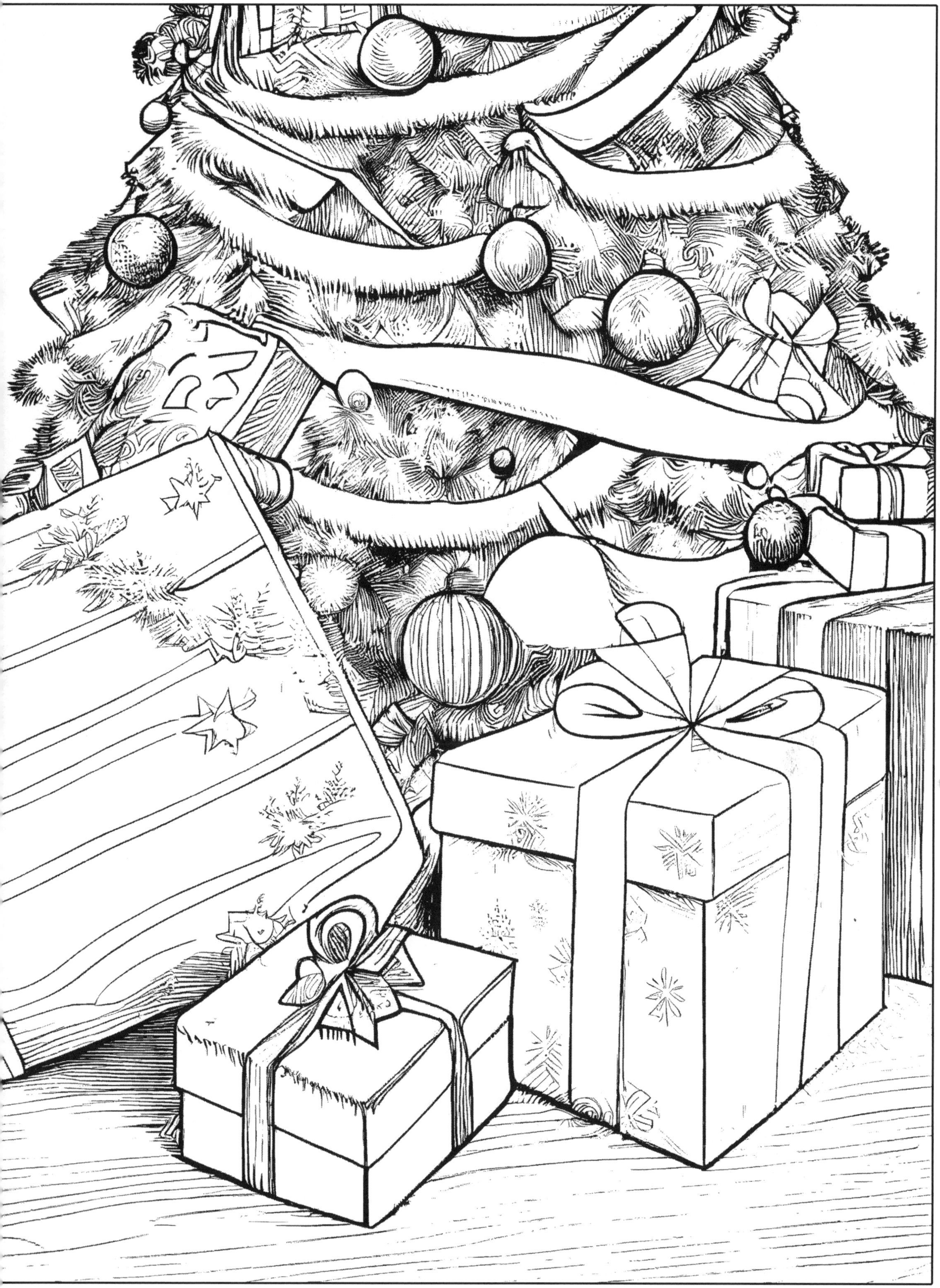

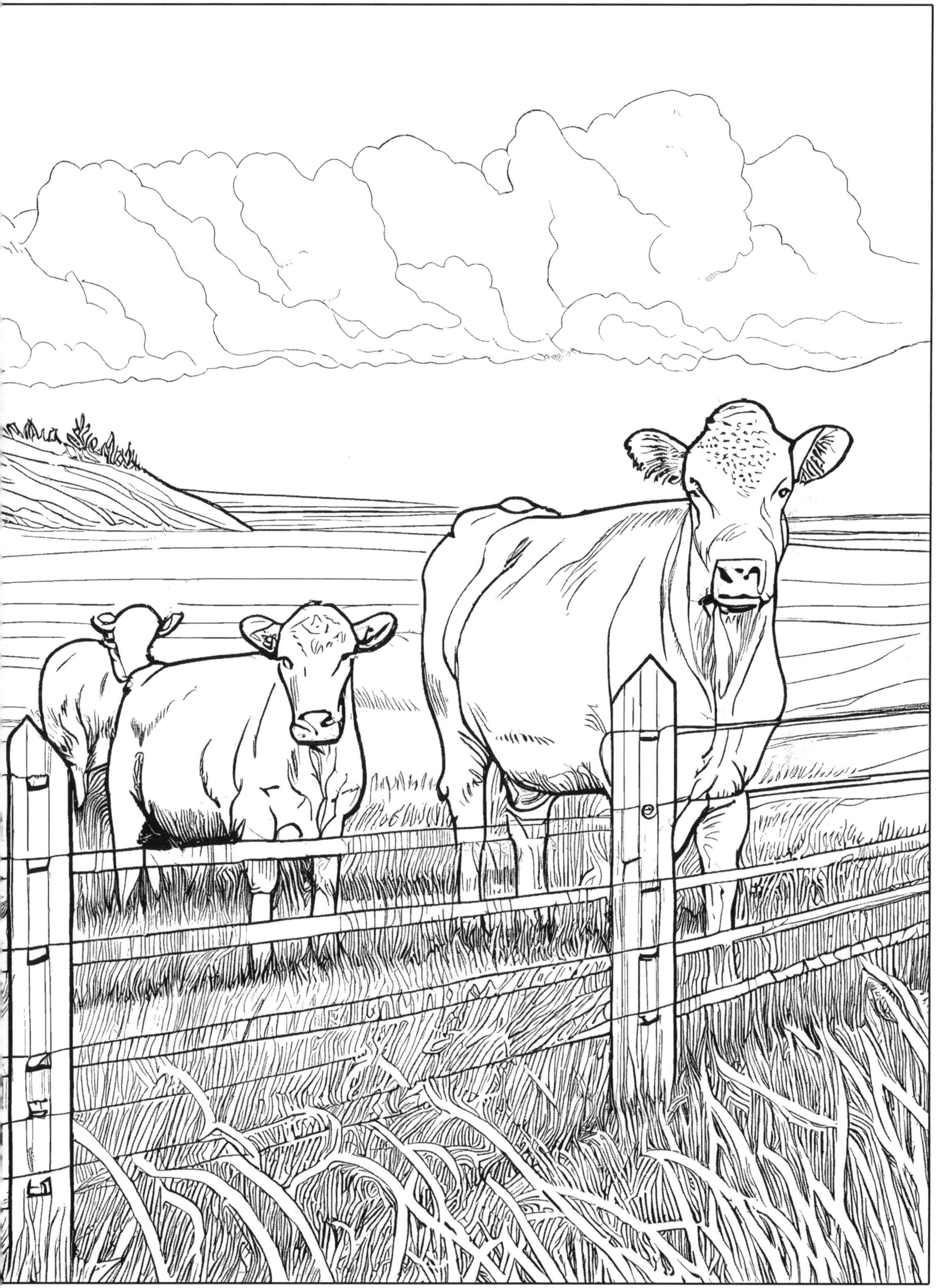

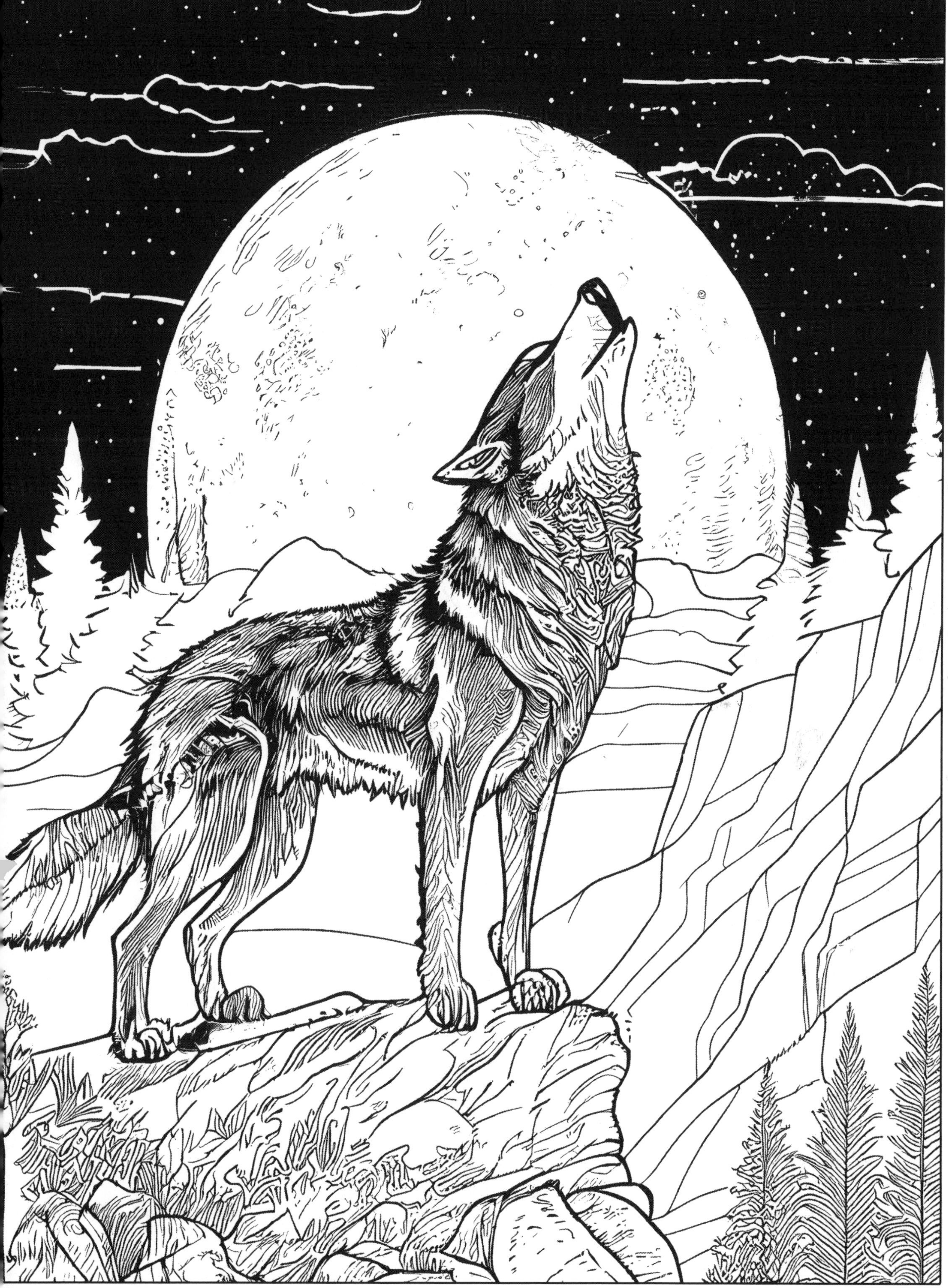

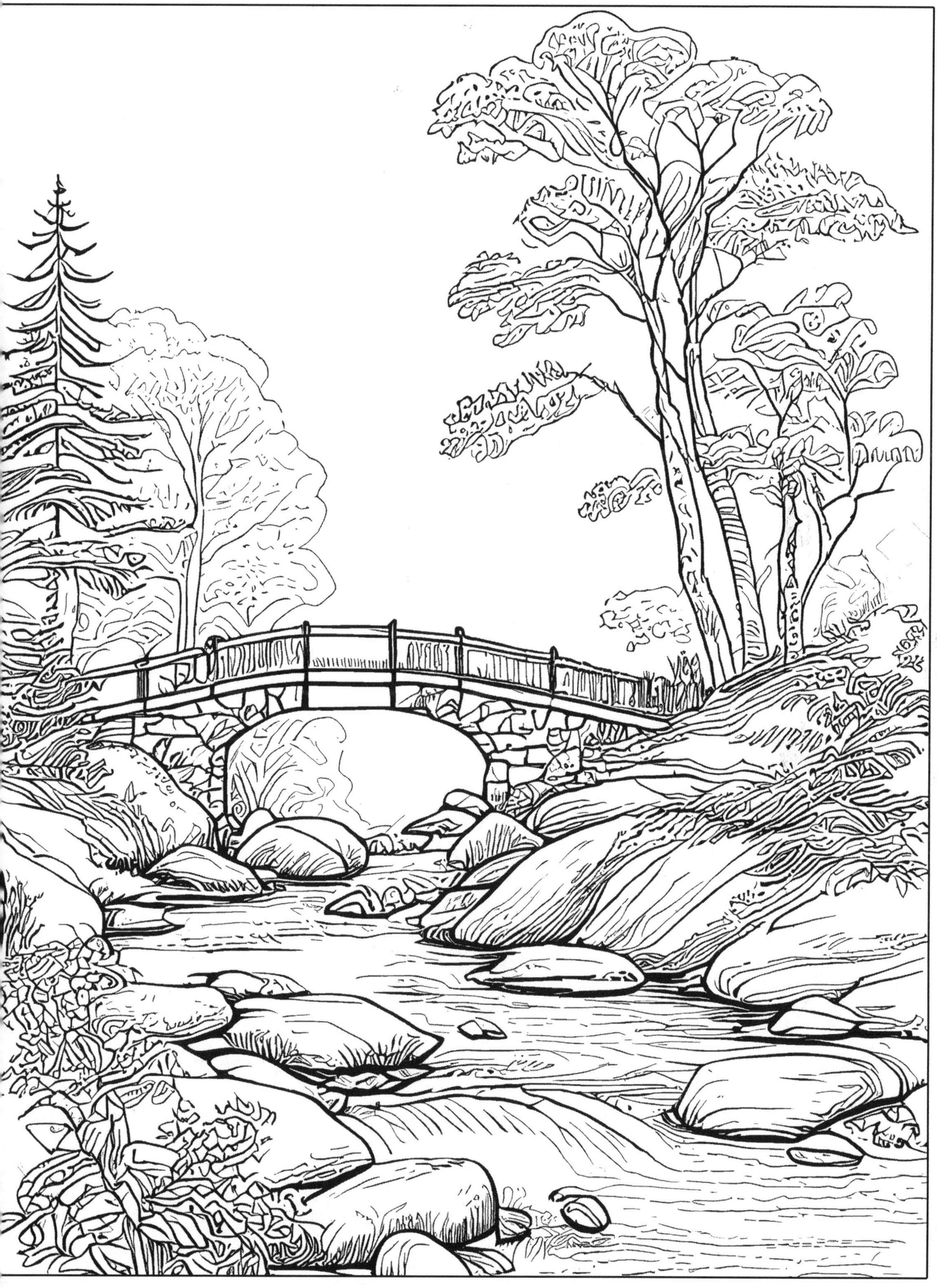

Made in United States
Orlando, FL
01 May 2023

32663953R00113